THE CIVILIZATION OF THE AMERICAN INDIAN SERIES

INDIAN ORATORY

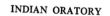

UNIVERSITY OF OKLAHOMA PRESS : NORMAN

W. C. Vanderwerth

Indian Oratory

FAMOUS SPEECHES BY NOTED INDIAN CHIEFTAINS

FOREWORD BY WILLIAM R. CARMACK

INTERNATIONAL STANDARD BOOK NUMBER: 0–8061–0948–3

LIBRARY OF CONGRESS CATALOG CARD NUMBER: 73–145502

Indian Oratory: Famous Speeches by Noted Indian Chieftains is Volume 110 in *The Civilization of the American Indian Series*.

Foreword

The oratory of a people reflects the major issues which concern them and the values which govern their decisions. In this time of renewed interest in American Indians, it is significant that little written record of their oratory exists, although Indians made much use of public address. Most of the accounts we do have are the heritage of the Indian's oral tradition. Some of the early white men who traveled and lived among the Indians left transcriptions of Indian tribal council meetings and speeches. From these scattered reports and the few other existing sources this book presents a reconstruction of contemporary thought of the leading men of many tribes.

Here for the first time the Indians' speeches are brought together in one book. The collection affords us a vivid picture of the issues facing the Indians from their point of view, presented by their leaders, who sought first to accommodate—and finally to resist—the engulfing tide of an alien society.

The conditions under which these speeches were delivered were generally adverse—the Indians usually at a decided disadvantage. The issues, as we see almost immediately, were not remote or abstract. They were of threatening and urgent concern —matters of life and death to a way of life as well as to individuals. Ultimately the question was whether to resort to forceful resistance or surrender a traditional way of life.

Around the council fires tribal affairs were settled without benefit of the written word, and young men attended so that they could hear the speeches, observe their delivery, and consider the weight of reasoned argument. Speakers at tribal councils were men of eminence in war or council or both. They were also men of dignity and ability, well trained in the oral tradition. Their speeches, which would do credit to any Athenian orator, should dispel for all time the myth of the Indian as ignorant savage. That these eloquent, moving speeches were often made with telling use of wit and sarcasm destroys the stereotype of the stoic, silent, humorless red man.

Each of these speeches was delivered without a prompter, without a speech writer, without a public-address system—with only the speaker's training, memory, and natural ability to aid him. The structure and form are sound, the use of literary devices is effective, and the messages are clear and poignant. The orators were well aware of the issues and knew that they were bargaining for nothing less than survival. That bargaining was carried out on battlefield and in council. The Indian's heroism on the battlefield is well known. Now in his speeches we can hear him and his no less heroic efforts in council.

WILLIAM R. CARMACK

Preface

In the wide-ranging search for material to include in this book many items have been read and reread until it is difficult to record just where the information was retrieved, or how many times some of it was found. A vast amount of data has been condensed into thumbnail biographies of the Indian orators and descriptions of the situations in which they made the selected speeches. Every effort was made to trace the speeches as far back as possible, so that little would be added or subtracted in the telling and retelling.

Thanks are offered to the publishers and authors who have permitted the use of material. The information included in "Sources" gives the speaker, the author, and the publisher of the work from which the chosen speech was taken.

Special thanks are due the librarians in the University of Oklahoma Library, and to the directors of the Phillips Collection and the Western History Collection of that library. The Oklahoma Historical Society and its Indian Archives Division have been the source of valuable material and pictures. Other historical societies, as well as the Bureau of American Ethnology, graciously complied to requests for data and pictures, and credit has been given in "Sources" for the material which was used.

W. C. VANDERWERTH

January 23, 1971

Contents

CONTENTS

xiv

CONTENTS

Illustrations

INDIAN ORATORY

Introduction

AN old yarn is told of a tourist passing through the West on a train, which stopped at a station to change the train crew. The pause gave passengers a chance to get out and walk about, and one interesting character they saw was an old Indian, reputed to have a phenomenal memory. The tourist thought he would test the old boy and asked, "What did you have for breakfast on the morning of October 9, 1904?"

The old Indian promptly replied, "Eggs!"

"Hah!" exclaimed the tourist. "You're safe enough on that —most of the people in the country have eggs for breakfast. You haven't proved anything to me."

Some years later the tourist made the same trip, and under the same circumstances saw the same old Indian. Thinking he would try another greeting to the old man, the tourist walked up, raised his hand, and said, "How!"

The old Indian looked up and said, "Scrambled."[1]

This story illustrates two points which are very important in considering the spoken word among the Indians of early America. Usually the Indians were brief and wasted few words, and their memory was extraordinary. They knew no written word, and they had to recall from memory everything they

[1] A. H. Verrill in his book *The Real Americans* has one version of this anecdote. I have heard several variations, and all of them probably have one source. Yarns seem to change with the telling, and finally often only faintly resemble the original.

talked about, having no notes as such to refresh their memory.

In their conference and council-fire sessions every man of valor and responsibility was given a chance to express himself. Each brave took his time in speaking, used many gestures, and sought approval of every important phrase. This procedure consumed time, and generally there was little opportunity to use superfluous words.

The Indians' greatest concern was that their movement around the countryside would be restricted, and that they would be confined to a small area or put into even smaller reservations. As soon as the Pilgrims landed at Plymouth their presence and its effect on the Indians' domain was evident. As the flood of immigrants increased, the anxiety of the Indians grew. The Indians objected strenuously to giving up any part of their territory. The whites seemed to think that whenever they moved in, the Indians should pull out and go into other sections of the country.

The Indians had deep roots in their respective areas, and had a fierce feeling of possession for their lands. This possessiveness was demonstrated even in intertribal relationships if one tribe encroached on the hunting territory of another. However, the Indians felt that the land belonged to all Indians, and upon this belief they more or less formed a united front in opposing settlement by the whites. They revered the land as Mother Earth, supplying all the things needed for a happy life. They felt that no tribe or individual had the right to cede any portion of the land, since all Indians were affected by the advance of white civilization and the loss of hunting territory.

Land was held under communal tenure, and any citizen of the agrarian tribes could cultivate as much land as he wished. Tribal laws protected him in his right of occupancy and in the possession of the improvements on the land. However, when he failed to use the land, title reverted to the nation. History confirms that the Indians were happy and prosperous under this form of ownership.

When the whites began their occupation of Indian lands, it was very difficult for the Indians to understand the idea of individual ownership of tracts of land and the manner in which the whites used and misused the land. This departure from tradition, to the Indians, bordered on the sacrilegious, and they were soon fighting viciously to repel the whites in the hope of recovering the land which they had lost. They wanted to prevent further expansion of the white settlements.

Most of the councils held between the whites and Indians were treaty sessions in which the principal objective was getting the Indians to give up more of their territory. Major General G. M. Dodge, who conducted many military campaigns against the Indians, expressed the opinion of many whites when he said, "The place to make a treaty is in the heart of their country, where we can dictate the terms; not they in our country."

Regardless of the friendly feeling which the Indians sometimes brought to the councils, they were forced to give up territory and finally were moved to the less desirable sections of the country, where it was impossible for them to exist as they had been accustomed to living for countless hundreds of years.

The resulting military campaigns, with the always increasing hordes of white settlers and pony soldiers, along with their muskets, breech-loading rifles, and, later, repeating rifles and artillery, soon had the Indians facing the grim possibility of annihilation. The peace talks which followed the military campaigns saw the Indians develop their oratorical abilities even further. The Indians tried eloquence instead of force in an effort to relieve their conditions. Leaders of the Indian tribes were taken to Washington to visit the Great White Father, and many were taken on to New York for visits designed to impress upon the "savages" the greatness of the land, and to let them see how

5

the whites lived, how many of them there were, and how futile it was for the Indian to continue resisting the white man's encroachment upon his land.

It must be realized that many of these speeches were translated, since the Indian orators often could not speak fluent English, or any at all. It is quite likely that the translations were very much as the speakers gave them, for the interpreters were trusted men and women, chosen because they could be depended upon, because they knew tribal language as well as English, and not because they could polish the wording of the speech as they gave the English version of what the Indian orator was saying. However, some of the Indians complained that the interpreters did not give a true explanation of what was said to the Indians and did not give the meaning which the Indians intended to convey when they were addressing the whites.

The Eastern tribes developed some outstanding speakers and statesmen. Historians may not have recorded the names of all the lesser speakers, but those whose names and orations have come down to us through the pages of history have been truly outstanding.

The tribes of the Great Plains were more mobile and of greater numbers than the Woodlands tribes. They also had to contend with graver problems and had a longer heritage of opposition to and hatred for the whites than did the New England and Eastern tribes. For this reason, more of them were adept at argument at the council fire and the treaty meeting. Many of these tribes had several men who could hold their own with any of the whites in a debate session.

Every one of the examples of Indian thought, opinion, and philosophy included in this collection has been chosen from actual speeches, made when the speakers were in front of an audience—either a tribal gathering or a peace council. None of the sometimes sparkling written communications of these gifted people have been included. In the case of the Indian orators, the speech was made without benefit of notes and came entirely from memory.

In some sections of the country wampum belts were used to help prompt the speaker. The belts of wampum were beautiful things, painstakingly and laboriously prepared. Colored beads of shell, bone, glass, and ceramic material were worked into designs which aided the orator in remembering the important subjects upon which he was speaking. The Indian speaker also had a memorized set of metaphors which he used in emphasizing his speech.

Francis Parkman's stupendous works on early American Indians reveals his interest in the First Americans. In writing about the use of wampum in speech making, he said:

An Indian council, on solemn occasions, is always opened with preliminary forms, sufficiently wearisome and tedious, but made indispensable by immemorial custom; for this people are as much bound by their conventional usages as the most artificial children of civilization. The forms are varied to some extent, according to the imagination and taste of the speaker; but in all essential respects they are closely similar throughout the tribes of Algonquin and Iroquois lineage. They run somewhat as follows, each sentence being pronounced with great solemnity, and confirmed by the delivery of a wampum belt: Brothers, with this belt I open your ears that you may hear—I remove grief and sorrow from your hearts—I draw from your feet the thorns which have pierced them as you journey thither—I clean the seats of the council-house, that you may sit at ease—I wash your head and body, that your spirits may be refreshed—I condole with you on the loss of the friends who have died since we last met—I wipe out any blood which may have been spilt between us.

The orator was careful in preparing his speech, and its effective delivery was enhanced by a good memory, and further emphasized by passing out belts of wampum at intervals to indicate sincerity on the part of the speaker.

The writer of one journal told of a Plains Indian chief who was attempting to impress neighboring tribes with his oratory and dedication to their welfare and his ability to lead them in warfare. He gave away horse after horse—wampum not being used in his area—until he was impoverished.

The wampum belts were strung on sinew, horse hair, or fine fiber, and while they did not have actual cash value, the belts were highly esteemed because of their beauty and the great amount of time required to make them. Wampum was occasionally used as a means of exchange by many tribes. The speaker came to the council fire supplied with belts of wampum which he passed after each important statement. Like the chief giving away his horses, the wampum giver could also literally bankrupt himself in his effort to convince his listeners of his sincerity.

In their splendid book *American Indian Mythology*, Alice Marriott and Carol K. Rachlin have preserved a wealth of ancient lore and explored the many facets of Indian poems, music, prayers, and oratory. They advance the thesis that the genius shared by the American Indian was and still remains "verbal and oral." The Indians delivered orations, composed poems and music and songs, and presented miracle plays which required days to complete.

Ritual prayers, often lasting for hours, had to be recited without error or the omission of a single syllable. The slightest deviation would interfere with the results sought through the ritual, and the Indians thought that any deviation might have a far-reaching effect upon the health, crops, hunting, and welfare of the people of the tribe. Young men attended council fires so they could observe, hear, and study the speeches and the method of delivery.

Some of the Indian orators came to be known as men who liked to hear their own voices and were ready to talk at any time, having scant regard for the effectiveness of their argument. No doubt they could have been accurately termed the windbags of the prairies. Some of those who had a reputation for talking long and saying little were maneuvered so they would not have much time to talk at important council fires. Probably it was a good thing that the passing of wampum belts was not the custom in those areas, or the speakers could not have afforded to present their arguments. Here one of our more or less modern terms could be applied—that "talk is cheap."

In considering Indian oratory many present-day followers of Western and Indian history think all too often of the old-time Indian as the grunt and "ugh" type, who waved his hands in some sort of sign language. Sign language was a very efficient method of communication under certain conditions, and was a necessity when language barriers had to be crossed. Ethnologists have divided the Indians into linguistic groups, but the tribes of some of these groups were so widely dispersed that many persons could not understand the language of all the members of their group. For this reason Indians developed the sign language and were able to carry on intelligent conversations with each other, no matter how widely their tribes were separated, or how different the linguistic groups.

A. H. Verrill in *The Real Americans* says that those familiar with the sign language of the Indians could converse as handily, as fluently, as comprehensively, and almost as rapidly, as by word of mouth. James McLaughlin, who worked among the Indians for many years, stated that his knowledge of the Sioux language, along with the use of the sign language, enabled him to carry on satisfactory conversation with most of the Indian tribes east of the Rocky Mountains and north of Texas. The whites were dependent upon interpreters for the sign language as well as the spoken word. Many white scouts and early-day trappers were adept in the use of the sign language.

Many of the harangues of the Indian leaders who have attempted to encourage, arouse, or pacify their peoples have been set down for record in various places. Most of these speeches are very smooth flowing, full of logic, and quite persuasive. Some of the Indian speakers were possibly better prepared to deliver their speeches than the whites who were their opposites in the council and treaty sessions.

It so happens that most of the speeches of which we have records deal with the Indians' conflict with the whites. The Indian leaders were trying to get their people to resist the whites, or making an attempt to get the Indians to try to live at peace with the white man. Many of the speeches have come from treaty sessions which resulted in the Indians surrendering everything they held dear—their land, hunting rights, and personal freedom—and submitting to life on the reservations.

Great effort was made to have the chiefs and leading warriors assemble for the conference, where the whites passed out gifts and trinkets as an indication that they were currying the Indians' favor and attention. The tone of the conference was then set with the delivery of a carefully prepared and written speech from the Great White Father. In most cases this was more in the form of an ultimatum than a message that sought to ease problems by some sort of arbitration.

Most of the Indians could not read the white man's word—or read any writing, for that matter—and they had to remember what had been said when their time came for rebuttal at the conferences.

Only two of the Indians' nations used even a form of record keeping. These records were the calendar histories of the Sioux and the Kiowas. The Kiowas, long associated with the Comanches in the Southwest, formerly ranged the Wyoming and Montana area, into which territory the Sioux had also moved. Some authorities suggest that the Sioux and Kiowas may have had close contact and that the Kiowa calendar may have developed after these people grasped the importance of the Sioux calendar.

These calendars, sometimes referred to as the "winter count," were skins upon which symbols and figures were drawn, one or a set of several on each skin for each year, depicting the outstanding event during the past twelve months. While the calendars were not actually a written record, by referring to their symbols the keepers of tribal history could more easily recall highlights of tribal activity and keep some count of the years as they passed. Contact with the whites was often noted in these calendars.

Many of the parleys between the Indians and whites revealed that the Indians had an uncanny ability to recall the exact conditions of peace treaties and would call the whites' attention to conditions which they had failed to observe. One instance was reported where the signed treaty was belatedly produced and it was found that the Indians were correct and the whites had been negligent while the Indians had scrupulously observed the specified conditions. The Indian speakers called upon their considerable oratorical skills in presenting a case for their people and for advancing their claims upon a universe which the Great Spirit had made and presented to them, with all its fruits and animals, pleasures and troubles, and the freedom to roam the untrammeled land—Mother Earth.

As sparkling as some of these orations were, the whites usually gave little attention to them at the time of delivery. This was graphically shown by Henry M. Stanley, correspondent for the *New York Times*, at the great Medicine Lodge Treaty Council in October, 1867. While the speech of Chief Ten Bears of the Comanches was being interpreted, Stanley looked around the group of participants, and wrote:

Harney, with head erect, watched with interest each dusky and painted face of the Indians around the tent. Sanborn picked his teeth and laughed jollily. Tappan read Indian reports about the destruction of the Indian village. Henderson with eyeglasses in his hand, seemed buried in deep study. Terry busied himself in printing alphabetical letters, and Augur whittled away with energy. Agent Leavenworth examined his children and made by-signals to old Satank, the oldest chief of the Kiowa Nation. The correspondents sat a la turque on the ground, their pencils flying over the paper.

Many writers explaining Indian history and describing living conditions have given at length the correspondence, orders, and speeches made by the whites in their drive toward containing, subjugating, and civilizing the Indian. Very few, even when the replies have been acknowledged, have done more than give excerpts from the responses by the Indians.

The spoken word of the Indian is of great interest and should be studied for a more complete understanding of the reaction of the Indians to a civilization which they could not understand. They had for many years enjoyed the power of strong nations, and had religious ideals of their own and a form of government which was effective for them. A vigorous search has resulted in a collection of the spoken word of the Indian participants in various council meetings; their orally delivered pleas for support from the tribes and the entreaties, threats, and replies the Indians made to the proposals from the whites.

Many of the speeches have been recorded only as excerpts. Others were taken down in full but have been so buried in archives as to be almost lost. It is hoped that these selections will help the reader envision the man making the speech and understand his feeling on the occasion. These men were giants in their times. They lived full lives as Indians whose way of life differed from that of the whites, but they performed deeds and spoke words which will be engraved on the face of history for all time. For every example included herein, there are dozens of other fine talks which are no less worthy of attention.

Aside from the futility of their efforts in behalf of their people it is tragic to note the way in which these men finished their stay on earth. Many were killed in battle, and there were suicides, burnings, stabbings, and poverty and neglect at the end of the road. Yet they were not the kind of men to evade anything, and when the end came they met it fearlessly.

The speeches have been arranged chronologically in order to give some idea of the problems faced by the Indians in meeting the ever-increasing infringement on their territories by the whites. Even in earliest colonial days the "savages" displayed a high degree of statesmanship and oratorical ability. Included are speeches by Indians from first contact with the whites, several from the last Great Council held on Medicine Lodge Creek in Kansas in 1867, and still others from less important councils in later years.

No known portrait of Teedyuscung has ever been recorded. There were some four or five portraits of the early Delaware Indians, but none of them were of this noted orator. Despite the lack of a portrait, two of his speeches are included in this selection. Teedyuscung appeared before the Colonial councils at every opportunity and spoke at great length on a wide range of subjects which related to the welfare and benefit of the Indians.

The following speech was made at the Statehouse in Philadelphia, Wednesday, March 15, 1758. William Denny, lieutenant governor, was presiding. Several Indians had accompanied Teedyuscung, and as he spoke he handed out belts of wampum to emphasize sections of his speech.

"I Gave the Halloo"

Brother: I hope your wise men of the Council and Assembly are now present to hear what we have to say. (Teedyuscung then taking out a large calumet pipe filled it with tobacco, and rising up said:)

Brother: The Governor and all your wise men present, hearken to what I am now going to say: At the Treaty at Easton, you desired me to hear you and publish what passed there to all the Indian Nations. I promised you to do it; I gave the halloo and published it to all the Indian Nations in this part of the world, even the most distant have heard me. The Nations to whom I published what passed between us have let me, Teedyuscung, know that they had heard and approved it, and, as I was about so good a work, they sent me this pipe, the same that their grandfathers used on such good occasions, and desired it might be filled with the same good tobacco, and that I, with my Brother, the Governor, would smoke it. They further assured me that if at any time I should perceive any dark clouds arise, and would smoke but two or three whiffs out of this pipe, these clouds would immediately disappear. (Teedyuscung then lighted the calumet pipe that was sent to them from the Indian Na-

16

tion, first smoked out of it himself, then gave to the Governor, who, with the Council and members of assembly, smoked it. Teedyuscung then proceeded, and taking hold of a long belt, wampum, said:)

Brother: I desire you would hear me, and I hope all who are present will attend to what I am going to say to the Governor.

Brother: I told you when we consulted together I would not do as had been done heretofore. I would not hide or conceal any part of it in my bosom, but would hold it up and publish it, that all the world may hear and see it, and this I shall ever continue to do.

Brother: You may remember I promised I would give a halloo; I have done it, and all the Nations you see represented by this belt, which I now hold in my hand, have heard whatever you and I have talked together when we were promoting the good work; I have made all these Nations as one man. All the Indian Nations from the Sun Rise to these beyond the Lakes, as far as the Sun sets, have heard what has passed between you and me and are pleased with it, and they have said to me, "Now, Brother Teedyuscung, we see that you and your brothers, the English, have been talking about what is good; we, therefore, send you this belt to let you know that we, the Nations who live some of us at the Sun Rise, and others at the Sun Set, have taken hold at the two ends of this belt, and we desire you and your brothers, the English, to take hold of the middle, and always, when you are consulting about what is good to hold it fast, as our lives and safety will entirely depend upon it." (As he was giving over the belt to the Governor, he further said:)

Now, Brother, the Governor: As Ten Nations joined before, and now eight more have taken hold of the covenant chain, we make, in all, now eighteen Nations who have hold of this belt.

Brother: Hear me, and all that are present take notice. You know I told you at Easton that all the power was in my hands, and as I held what was good in my hand, I told you I would hold it up, and if I saw any that were willing to live quietly and peaceably, I would deliver it into their hands, and all the world should see to whom I did deliver it.

Brother: I am heard now by all Indians, and they are pleased, and have said to me, Brother Teedyuscung, you are promoting what is good; we have looked and enquired who has been the cause of the darkness; there are three concerned, English, French and Indians. We have found one of these three have been the cause of it, and he shall die. (After a pause, Teedyuscung said something was forgot, and added that the man is a Frenchman.)

Brother: There is a good deal of news going backwards and forwards, but though it be so, I have stopped his ears and blinded his eyes, so that the news runs right before his breast, he shall hear nothing of it, that is, though the Indians who have joined me live behind the French, must pass by them to come to us, yet they shall know nothing of what passes between us.

Now, Brother, as I have blinded the eyes of the French and stopped their ears, I hope you will do the same. (He gave a belt of 12 rows.)

Brother, and all present attend to what I am going to say:

You may remember you told me I was so capable a man as you were; I see you tell true, you are really a greater man than I, and these words encouraged me. I have also received encouragement from the Indian Nations. Now, Brother, press on with all your might in promoting the good work we are engaged in; let us beg the God that made us to bless our endeavors, and I am sure if you exert yourselves, and God will grant a blessing, we shall live. (He passed a belt of eight rows.)

Brother, the Governor, and all present: The Indians who live back encourage you and me; they have seen us hold councils together, and they press us on to execute what we have begun.

They have said to me: "Do you, Teedyuscung, and your brothers press on and don't be discouraged. It is a work of great moment which you have undertaken. When you begin a great work you can't expect to finish it all at once; therefore do you and your brothers press on, and let nothing discourage you till you have entirely finished what you have begun." Now, Brother, as for me, I assure you I will press on, and the contrary winds may blow strong in my face, yet I will go forwards and never turn back, but continue to press forward until I have finished, and I would have you do the same.

Brother: One word more; I earnestly desire you to press on; let us proceed in the good road and finish the work we have undertaken. I desire you would open and clear your eyes and look upon our wives and children with pity and compassion, and finish the work as soon as you can. Though you may hear birds singing on this side and that side, you must not take notice of that, but hear me when I speak to you, and lay it to heart, for you may always depend that what I say shall be true. (Teedyuscung gave a belt of seven rows, then arose and taking the hand of the Governor, said:)

At present I have no more to say, but when I hear any news you shall hear it, for your ear and mine are one.

On Saturday, September 13, 1760, Teedyuscung returned to Philadelphia from a trip to the Ohio country, where he visited some of the Delaware Indians. He visited the governor that day, and asked for a hearing and that was arranged for Monday, September 15. James Hamilton, lieutenant governor, along with several other citizens received Teedyuscung, who was accompanied by several other Delawares. Again, as his talk progressed, Teedyuscung handed over strings and belts of wampum to emphasize points in his speech and to indicate his sincerity.

Here is what was recorded in the Colonial Records of Pennsylvania. The spelling of the council scribe has been retained.

19

"All Their Warriors Have Made
Themselves as One Man"

Brother: I have nothing to say to you of my own at this time; I shall only tell you some news; you may remember that I often promised you to give the Hallo thro' all the Indian Nations. I have been a long way back, a great way indeed, beyond the Allegheny, among my friends there; when I got as far as the Salt Lick Town, towards the head of Beaver Creek, I stopped there and sent messengers to the chiefs of all the Indians in those parts, desiring them to come and hold council; it took three weeks to collect them together, and then, having a large number gathered together, I communicated to them all that has passed between me and this Government for four years past, at which they were glad, and declared that this was the first time they had had a right understanding of these transactions; they said they heard every now and then, that we were sitting together about peace, but they were not acquainted 'till now with the particulars of our several conferences; I concealed nothing from them, and when they had heard all they were right glad. It gave joy to their very hearts. (He handed out a string, and then holding a belt in his hand, he proceeded:)

Brother: This belt came from an Indian Nation, the Kicka-bouses, who live a great way beyond the Twicktwees; by it they told me that it was the first time they had heard of my making peace with the English; that they were greatly pleased with it, and joined their hands heartily to it, and they would all agree to what their Grandfathers, the Delawares, should conclude with the English; they likewise desired me to let the Governor know that tho' they lived a great way off, further than the other Na-tions, yet they would come with them in the spring, and hold council at Philadelphia. (A belt.)

Brother: My son, Amos, sitting there is a warrior and captain.

I took him along with me, and at this great meeting of Indians, I gave him a belt to speak to the warriors, as from me to join in the peace. So after the old men had done holding council the warriors went by themselves and held a council together; and when this was over they made a speech to us old men, in which they assured us that they had consulted together, and agreed as one man to every thing that we had concluded upon, and would heartily keep the peace; that they pitied the old men, women and children; and tho' they had hitherto kept their hands shut, yet they would now open them, and no longer keep the English flesh and blood within their hands, but open them and set all the prisoners at liberty. (A string.)

Brother: As I went along that part of the country where the Munsies now live, I took along with me this young man (pointing to a brave). He is the son of their principal man and was very willing to go, having a desire to hear what should be said on all sides. After the general council was over, he was mightyly pleased with it, and in order to enable him to relate faithfully all that has passed, and to use his influence, that all his Nation might concur in it, I gave him two Belts and Eight Fathom of wampum. I had a particular reason for doing so, because I knew that their Nation had taken many prisoners, and that they detained them in their towns; so I thought this would incline him to get them delivered up. (A belt.)

Brother: You know that we have been sitting together these four years past. All the Indian Nations back, yea, a great way back, have heard all the particulars that have passed between us. All their chiefs and all their warriors have made themselves as one man, and have formed their hands to our peace, and promise never to break it, but to hold the peace belt fast. The warriors have agreed to confirm what the old men have done. In consequence of this, I assure you no one Nation shall hereafter quarrel with you or with one another, without its being first determined in a General Indian Council, at which it is agreed that the English shall be present. This is the unanimous determination of all the Indian Nations that I have seen, viz.: the Tarons, the Nelametenos or Owendaots, the Twicktwees, the Shawonese, the Chippaways, all the tribes of the Delawares and others, to the number of ten Nations, all principal Nations of those who live far back to the westward; they have all agreed to what has been said on the belts and strings, which I have now delivered. (A string.)

Brother: This is all I have to say at this time. Tomaquior, the Beaver King (who is the head man of the Delawares at the Ohio), did not give me anything in charge to say to the Governor. We were all present in the great council at Pittsburg, and heard him tell the General that he would go to Philadelphia in the summer, and hold a council with this Government, in complyance with the several invitations he had received from it. I told Tomaqui that Pittsburg was no place to hold council, as that the Old Fire was here; that Pittsburg was only a place for warriors to speak in, and that he should do no council business in Pittsburg. And accordingly Tomaqui told the General that he would not say any thing to him, but say it at the place where their grandfathers were always used to hold council with the English.

Brother: This is all. I think to come and visit you tomorrow, and to talk over many things that I have seen in my journey.

Pontiac, Ottawa, born 1720; died April, 1769. This illustration is a photograph of a painting made by Sue Holmes Smith, daughter of Norman G. Holmes, long-time employee of the Indian Service and a descendant of Pontiac.

Pontiac

PONTIAC has been the subject of many writers, and his movement across the pages of history has been thoroughly documented. His influence among the Ottawas and other tribes of colonial days was tremendous. He was an outstanding leader and a gifted speaker, and was able to perform to good advantage in any setting.

Francis Parkman was one of the earliest writers to cover thoroughly the activities of Pontiac, and his research and writings were extensive. Pontiac was born in 1720 near the present Fort Wayne, Indiana, on the Maumee River, at the mouth of the Auglaize, where the city of Defiance is now located.

Pontiac and his Ottawas once paid homage to the French as being their friends and the French king as being their Great Father. Pontiac was concerned about the English settlers taking Indian lands, and worked to get French help in his war against the colonists.

Pontiac was killed at Cahokia, Illinois, in April, 1769, by a drunken Indian who had been bribed by a trader with a barrel of whisky to do the act. Later evaluation of Pontiac's activities indicates his influence was of less importance than it had previously appeared.

The first speech below is an allegorical presentation in which Pontiac was trying to inspire confidence in his plan for resistance by resorting to the mysterious and relating it to action against the colonists. In the story he tells, the god advises the Indian brave to put less reliance upon trade goods and to resist in any way the influx of white settlers. The speech was made at a council at the River Ecores on April 27, 1763, before the seige of Detroit.

A second speech is included in which Pontiac makes an about-face and requests more supplies and ammunition from the whites so that the Indians can secure food.

A Delaware Indian conceived an eager desire to learn wisdom from the Master of Life; but, being ignorant where to find him, he had recourse to fasting, dreaming, and magical incantations. By these means it was revealed to him, that, by moving forward in a straight, undeviating course, he would reach the abode of the Great Spirit. He told his purpose to no one, and having provided the equipments of a hunter—gun, powder-horn, ammunition, and a kettle for preparing his food—he set out on his errand. For some time he journeyed on in high hope and confidence. On the evening of the eighth day, he stopped by the side of a brook at the edge of a meadow, where he began to make ready his evening meal, when, looking up, he saw three large openings in the woods before him, and three well-beaten paths which entered them. He was much surprised; but his wonder increased, when, after it had grown dark, the three paths were more clearly visible than ever. Remembering the important object of his journey, he could neither rest nor sleep; and, leaving his fire, he crossed the meadow, and entered the largest of the three openings. He had advanced but a short distance into the forest, when a bright flame sprang out of the ground before him, and arrested his steps. In great amazement, he turned back, and entered the second path, where the same wonderful phenomenon again encountered him; and now, in terror and bewilderment, yet still resolved to persevere, he took the last of the three paths. On this he journeyed a whole day without interruption, when at length, emerging from the forest, he saw before him a vast mountain, of dazzling whiteness. So precipitous was the ascent that the Indian thought it hopeless to go farther, and looked around him in despair; at that moment, he saw, seated at some distance above, the figure of a beautiful woman arrayed in white, who arose as he looked upon her, and thus accosted him:

26

"How can you hope, encumbered as you are, to succeed in your design? Go down to the foot of the mountain, throw away your gun, your ammunition, your provisions, and your clothing; wash yourself in the stream which flows there, and you will then be prepared to stand before the Master of Life."

The Indian obeyed, and again began to ascend among the rocks, while the woman, seeing him still discouraged, laughed at his faintness of heart, and told him that, if he wished for success, he must climb by the aid of one hand and one foot only. After great toil and suffering, he at length found himself at the summit. The woman had disappeared, and he was left alone. A rich and beautiful plain lay before him, and at a little distance he saw three great villages, far superior to the squalid wigwams of the Delawares. As he approached the largest, and stood hesitating whether he should enter, a man gorgeously attired stepped forth, and, taking him by the hand, welcomed him to the celestial abode. He then conducted him into the presence of the Great Spirit, where the Indian stood confounded at the unspeakable splendor which surrounded him. The Great Spirit bade him be seated, and thus addressed him:

"I am the Maker of heaven and earth, the trees, lakes, rivers, and all things else. I am the Maker of mankind; and because I love you, you must do my will. The land on which you live I have made for you, and not for others. Why do you suffer the white men to dwell among you? My children, you have forgotten the customs and traditions of your forefathers. Why do you not clothe yourselves in skins, as they did, and use the bows and arrows, and the stone-pointed lances, which they used? You have bought guns, knives, kettles, and blankets, from the white men, until you can no longer do without them; and, what is worse, you have drunk the poison fire-water, which turns you into fools. Fling all these things away; live as your wise fore-fathers lived before you. And as for these English—these dogs dressed in red, who have come to rob you of your hunting-grounds, and drive away the game—you must lift the hatchet against them. Wipe them from the face of the earth, and then you will win my favor back again, and once more be happy and prosperous. The children of your great father, the King of France, are not like the English. Never forget that they are your brethren. They are very dear to me, for they love the red men, and understand the true mode of worshipping me."

. . .

The speech continues at some length, in which Pontiac passed on ideas of religion and morality which were intended to inspire the council members into action against the British. The word was to be passed on to all villages and the Indian brave was to have been the messenger.

The second speech made by Pontiac was given at a meeting at Fort Detroit in August of 1765. The fortunes of the French and the Indians had completely changed, and Pontiac had made peace with the British. In this talk to the military representatives he seeks relief for his people. During the progress of the talk, Pontiac presented several belts of wampum to the representative of the crown, emphasizing the points which he had made in his speech.

In the first speech Pontiac presents his case for opposition to the British through the allegory of the Indians' reliance upon the new-fangled goods and equipment, but here he plainly asks for the guns and powder of which he had spoken lightly earlier.

Croghan's Journal in *Illinois Historical Collections* shows a footnote stating that about thirty chiefs and five hundred warriors attended this council. This was the last major transaction involving Pontiac and the English.

"Father, Be Strong and Take Pity on Us, Your Children, as Our Former Father Did"

Father, we have all smoked out the pipe of peace. It's your children's pipe, and as the war is all over, and the Great Spirit and giver of light, who has made the Earth and everything therein, has brought us all together this day for our mutual good to promote the good works of peace. I declare to all nations that I had settled my peace with you before I came here, and now deliver my pipe to be sent to Sir William Johnson, that he may know I have made peace and taken the King of England for my father, in the presence of all the nations now assembled; and whenever any of those nations go to visit him, they may smoke out of it with him in peace.

Father, we are obliged to you for lighting up our old council fire for us, and desiring us to return to it, but we are now settled on the Maumee River, not far from hence. Whenever you want us you will find us there ready to wait on you. The reason I choose to stay where we are now settled is that we love liquor, and did we live here as formerly, our people would be always drunk, which might occasion some quarrels between the soldiers and them. This, Father, is all the reason I have for not returning to our old settlements, and that we live so nigh this place that when we want to drink, we can easily come for it.

Father, be strong and take pity on us, your children, as our former Father did. 'Tis just the hunting season of your children. Our Fathers, the French, formerly used to credit his children for powder and lead to hunt with. I request in behalf of all the nations present that you will speak to the traders now here to do the same. My Father, once more I request you will take pity on us, and tell your traders to give your children credit for a little powder and lead, as the support of our families depend upon it.

29

We have told you where we live, that whenever you want us and let us know it, we will come directly to you.

Father, you stopped up the rum barrel when we came here, 'till the business of this meeting was over. As it is now finished, we request you may open the barrel that your children may drink and be merry.

Cornplanter, Seneca, born 1732–1740; died February 18, 1836.

Cornplanter

CORNPLANTER was one of the great Indian orators in the late 1700's and early 1800's. He was a rival of Red Jacket, another Seneca, but Cornplanter was born before the birth of Red Jacket, and he lived several years after Red Jacket died. The birth date of Cornplanter, or Ki-on-twog-ky, has not been definitely determined, but it was between 1732 and 1740. He was born at Connewaugus, on the Genesee River in New York. His mother was a fullblood Seneca, and his father is thought to have been an Irishman named O'Bail. The name has sometimes been used as O'Beale, and Cornplanter has been referred to as John O'Beale.

Cornplanter was active as a chief of the Senecas. He signed many treaties, including those made at Fort Stanwix in 1784, and others in 1789, 1797, and 1802. In 1790 he went to Philadelphia to lay his complaints before George Washington. He had made an earlier trip to England, and while there had taken up English dress and mannerisms. Upon his return his tribesmen tore off his fancy clothes, dressed him in traditional garb, and applied customary greases to his body.

Cornplanter frequently attended councils in Philadelphia, traveling great distances for these sessions, in order to protest treatment of his Indians and make peaceful attempts to secure better conditions. He died February 18, 1836, at more than ninety years of age. Some authorities set his age at one hundred years.

The following speech was made at council in Philadelphia on October 29, 1790, and is quite lengthy. It relates mistreatment of his people, and in conciliatory manner asks action to relieve the Indians' conditions. Note the reference to the whites as "Father." This was not often used, the Indians preferring a more equal basis,

33

and frequently using "Brother" in their council speeches. Five of his tribesmen accompanied him and appeared with him at the council. He started his talk with a short "invocation."

"Listen to Me, Fathers of the Thirteen Fires"

The Fathers of the Quaker State, Obeale or Cornplanter, returns thanks to God for the pleasure he has in meeting you this day with six of his people.

Fathers: Six years ago I had the pleasure of making peace with you, and at that time a hole was dug in the earth, and all contentions between my nation and you ceased and were buried there.

At a treaty then held at Fort Stanwix between the six nations of Indians and the Thirteen Fires, three friends from the Quaker State came to me and treated with me for the purchase of a large tract of land upon the northern boundary of Pennsylvania, extending from Tioga to Lake Erie for the use of their warriors. I agreed to sale of the same, and sold it to them for four thousand dollars. I begged of them to take pity on my nation and not buy it forever. They said they would purchase it forever, but that they would give me further one thousand dollars in goods when the leaves were ready to fall, and when I found that they were determined to have it, I agreed that they should have it. I then requested, as they were determined to have the land to permit my people to have the game and hunt upon the same, which request they complied with, and promised me to have it put upon record, that I and my people should have that privilege.

Fathers: The six nations then requested that another talk might be held with the Thirteen Fires, which was agreed to, and a talk afterwards held between them at Muskingum. Myself with three of my chiefs attended punctually, and were much fatigued in endeavoring to procure the attendance of the other nations, but none of them came to the council fire except the Delawares and the Wyandots.

Fathers: At the same treaty the Thirteen Fires asked me on which side I would die, whether on their side, or the side on those nations who did not attend the council fire. I replied, listen to me fathers of the Thirteen Fires, I hope you will consider how kind your fathers were treated by our fathers, the six nations, when they first came into this country, since which time you have become strong, insomuch, that I now call you fathers.

In former days when you were young and weak, I used to call you brother, but now I call you father. Father, I hope you will take pity on your children, for now I inform you that I'll die on your side. Now, father, I hope you will make my bed strong.

Fathers of the Quaker State: I speak but little now, but will speak more when the Thirteen Fires meet, I will only inform you further, that when I had finished my talk with the Thirteen Fires, General Gibson, who was sent by the Quaker State, came to the fire, and said that the Quaker State had bought of the Thirteen Fires a tract of land extending from the northern boundary of Pennsylvania at Connewango River to Buffaloe Creek on Lake Erie, and thence along the said lake to the northern boundary of Pennsylvania aforesaid. Hearing this I run to my father, and said to him, father have you sold this land to the Quaker State, and he said he did not know, it might have been done since he came there. I then disputed with Gibson and Butler, who was with him about the same, and told them I would be satisfied if the line was run from Connewango River through Chatochque Lake to Lake Erie, for Gibson and Butler had told me that the Quaker State had purchased the land from the Thirteen Fires, but that notwithstanding the Quaker State had given to me one thousand dollars in fine prime goods which were ready for me and my people at Fort Pitt, we then agreed that the line should be run from Connewango River through Chatochque Lake into Lake

Erie, and that one-half of the fish in Chatochque Lake should be mine and one-half theirs.

They then said as the Quaker State had purchased the whole from the Thirteen Fires, that the Thirteen Fires must pay back to the Quaker State the value of the remaining land. When I heard this my mind was at ease, and I was satisfied.

I then proposed to give a half mile square of land upon the line so agreed upon to a Mr. Hartzhorn who was an ensign in General Harmar's army out to a Mr. Britt, a cadet who acted as a clerk upon occasion, and who I well know by the name of Half-Town, for the purpose of their settling there to prevent any mischief being committed in future upon my people's lands, and I hoped that the Quaker State would in addition thereto give them another half mile square on their side of the line so agreed upon for the same purpose, expecting thereby that the line so agreed upon would be known with sufficient certainty and that no disputes would thereafter arise between my people and the Quaker State concerning it. I then went to my father of the Thirteen Fires and told him I was satisfied, and the coals being covered up I said to my children you must take your course right through the woods to Fort Pitt. When I was leaving Muskingum my own son who remained a little while behind to warm himself at the fire was robbed of a rifle by one of the white men, who, I believe, to have been a Yankee. Myself with Mr. Joseph Nicholson and a Mr. Morgan then travelled three days together through the wilderness, but the weather being very severe they were obliged to separate from me, and I sent some of my own people along with Mr. Nicholson and Mr. Morgan as guides to conduct them on to Wheelen.

After I had separated from Mr. Nicholson and Mr. Morgan, I had under my charge one hundred and seventy persons of my own nation, consisting of men, women and children to conduct through the wilderness through heaps of briars, and having lost our way, we, with great difficulty reached Wheelen. When arrived there being out of provision I requested of a Mr. Zanes to furnish me and my people with bacon and flour to the amount of seventeen dollars, to be paid for out of goods belonging to me and my people at Fort Pitt. Having obtained my request, I proceeded on my journey for Pittsburg, and about ten miles from Wheelen my party were fired upon by three white people, and one of my people in the rear of my party received two shot through his blanket.

Fathers: It was a constant practice with me throughout the whole journey to take great care of my people, and not suffer them to commit any outrages or drink more than their necessities required. During the whole of my journey only one accident happened which was owing to the kindness of the people of the town called Catfish, in the Quaker State, who, while I was talking with the head men of the town, gave to my people more liquor than was proper, and some of them got drunk, which obliged me to continue there with my people all night, and in the night my people were robbed of three rifles and one shot gun; and though every endeavor was used by the head men of the town upon complaint made to them to discover the perpetrators of the robbery, they could not be found; and on my people's complaining to me I told them it was their own fault by getting drunk.

Fathers: Upon my arrival at Fort Pitt I saw the goods which I had been informed of at Muskingum, and one hundred of the blankets were all moth eaten and good for nothing, I was advised not to take the blankets, but the blankets which I and my people then had being all torn by the briars in our passage through the wilderness, we were under the necessity of taking them to keep ourselves warm; and what most surprised me, was that after I had received the goods they extinguished the fire and swept away the ashes, and having no interpreter there I could talk with no

37

one upon the subject. Feeling myself much hurt upon the occasion, I wrote a letter to you Fathers of the Quaker State, complaining of the injury, but never received any answer. Having waited a considerable time, and having heard that my letter got lost, I wrote a second time to you Fathers of the Quaker State and then I received an answer.

I am very thankful to have received that answer, and as the answer intreated me to come and speak for myself, I thank God that I have this opportunity, I therefore speak to you as follows. I hope that you, the Fathers of the Quaker State, will fix some person at Fort Pitt to take care of me and my people. I wish, and it is the wish of my people if agreeable to you that my present interpreter, Joseph Nicholson, may be the person, as I and my people have a confidence in him, and are satisfied that he will always exert himself to preserve peace and harmony between you and us. My reasons for wishing an interpreter to be placed there, are that often times when my hunters and people come there, their canoes and other things are stolen, and they can obtain no redress, not having any person there on whom they can rely to interpret for them and see justice done to them.

Fathers of the Quaker State: About a year ago a young man, one of my tribe who lived among the Shawanese, was one of a party who had committed some outrages and stolen a quantity of skins the property of David Duncan, being at Fort Pitt, was seized by the white people there who would have put him into confinement and perhaps to death had not some of the chiefs of the Seneca Nation interfered and bound themselves to the said David Duncan, who insisted upon satisfaction, for payment of the sum of five hundred and thirty dollars for the said skins so stolen, upon which the young man aforesaid was released and delivered up to them.

Fathers of the Quaker State: I wish now to acquaint you with what happened to one of my people about four years ago, four miles above Fort Pitt: A young man who was married to my wife's sister, when he was hunting, was murdered by a white man. There were three reasons for his being killed: In the first place he had a very fine riding horse; secondly, he was very richly dressed, and had about him a good deal of silver; and thirdly, he had with him a very fine rifle. The white man invited him to his house, to light from his horse, and as he was getting off his horse, his head being rather down, the white man struck him with a tomahawk on the head and killed him, and having plundered him dragged him into the river. Upon discovery of the murder, my people, with Mr. Nicholson and Mr. Duncan, had a great deal of trouble, and took a great deal of pains to find out the person who had committed the murder, and after three days' searching, they discovered him.

Father of the Quaker State: About five years ago, one of my chiefs, name Half Town, was sent to Fort Pitt to deliver up into your hands your own flesh and blood who were taken in the war, and before he returned two horses were stolen from him by the white people. Now, Fathers, I will inform you of another accident which happened to my people last winter, fifteen miles below Fort Pitt. My nephew, with a hunting party, being there, was shot through the head in Mr. Nicholson's camp, the particulars of which Mr. Nicholson, who is here present, can inform you.

Well, Fathers, I beg of you once more not to let such bad people be 'longside of me. And, Fathers, you must not think I or any of my people are bad or wish evil to you and yours, nor must you blame us for mischiefs that have been committed by the other nations. Fathers, consider me and my people, and the many injuries we have sustained by the repeated robberies, and in the murders and depredations committed by the whites against us.

It is my wish and the wishes of my people to live peaceably

and quietly with you and yours, but the losses we have sustained require some compensation. I have, with the consent of my people, agreed to receive from you eight hundred and thirty dollars, as a satisfaction for all losses and injuries I and my people have sustained, and this being paid me by you, to enable me to satisfy such of my people as have sustained those losses and suffered those injuries, we shall, I hope, in future live peaceable together, and bury in the earth all ill will and enmity to each other.

Fathers of the Quaker State: I have now had the pleasure to meet you with six of my people. We have come a great way, by your desire, to talk with you and to show to you the many injuries my nation has sustained. It now remains with you to do with me and my people what you please, on account of the present trouble which I and my people have taken for your satisfaction, and in compliance with your request.

Fathers, having come this great way at your request, and as it is necessary for some of us to remain here to talk with the Thirteen Fires when they meet, I have concluded to send back four of my people, and to remain here myself with Half Town and my interpreter, Mr. Nicholson, until that time, which I hope you will approve of. But should you not approve of it, I must be under the necessity of returning with the whole of my people, which will be attended with a considerable expense.

Fathers of the Quaker State: You have now got the most of our lands, and have taken the game upon the same. We have only the privilege of hunting and fishing thereon. I, therefore, would make this further request, that a store may be established at Fort Pitt for the accommodation of my people and the other nations when they go out to hunt; and where they may purchase goods at a reasonable price. For, believe me, Fathers, you yourselves would be frightened were you to know the extravagant prices we are obliged to pay for the goods we purchase.

There is a man (Esquire Wilkie) in Pittsburg, who has taken a great deal of pains to serve my people, and has pitied them; my people, when there, are very kindly treated by him, and give him a great deal of trouble, but he thinks nothing of it; he is the man my people wish should have charge of the store.

Fathers of the Quaker State: I have heard that you have been pleased to present to me a tract of land, but as yet I have not seen no writings for the same; well, Fathers, if it is true that you have given me this tract of land, I can only thank you for the same, but I hope you will also give me tools and materials for working the same.

Fathers of the Quaker State: Five years ago, when I used to be with my present interpreter, Joseph Nicholson, he took care of me and my people. Considering his services and the difficulties he underwent in his journey from Muskingum to Fort Pitt, the Six Nations wished to have him seated upon a tract of land of six miles square, lying in the forks of Allegany River, and Broken Straw creek, and accordingly patented the same to him, this being the place where the battle was fought between my people and yours, and where about thirty of my people were beaten by him and twenty-five of your people, and where he was shot through the thigh. Now, Fathers, it is my wish, and I tell you it is the wish of the whole Six Nations, in behalf of whom and myself, I request that you would grant and confirm to our brother and friend, the before named Joseph Nicholson, the aforesaid tract of land, as described in our patent or grant to him.

This, Fathers, is all I have to say to the Quaker State, and I hope you will consider well all I have mentioned.

Red Jacket, Seneca, born about 1756; died January 20, 1830.

Red Jacket

RED JACKET was asked what he had done to distinguish himself as a warrior among the Seneca Indians, and he replied: "A warrior? I am an orator! I was born an orator!" The Seneca chief's tribal name was Sa-Go-Ye-Wat-Ha, or He-keeps-them-awake, and may have been appropriate for his description as an orator, for he certainly was gifted in his ability to speak at council fires, treaty sessions, and before governmental agencies. His name of Red Jacket is attributed to the persistent wearing of a red military jacket given him by a British army officer.

Red Jacket was born about 1752 in the vicinity of Lake Geneva, New York, near Seneca Lake. He had distinguished himself in war, and that he made a mark for himself oratorically cannot be denied. William L. Stone in his book, *The Life and Times of Sa-Go-Ye-Wat-Ha, or Red Jacket*, has collected many of the speeches of Red Jacket, and has given the conditions under which they were delivered. Red Jacket died January 20, 1830, at seventy-eight.

Red Jacket made a trip to Washington, D.C., in 1792, at the invitation of President George Washington, who wished to impress upon him the futility of opposing the numerical strength and abilities of the whites. He dined with President Washington, and on March 26 addressed the United States Senate, where he stressed the importance of satisfying the Indian tribes with the good faith and liberality of the whites. Red Jacket spent several weeks in Washington, transacting business which concerned the Senecas and other Indian tribes.

The speech given here was at a conference at which other Seneca chiefs were present, and Red Jacket is replying to the offers of the whites to bring their religion to the Indians.

Friend and Brother! It was the will of the Great Spirit that we should meet together this day. He orders all things, and he has given us a fine day for our council. He has taken his garment from before the sun and has caused the bright orb to shine with brightness upon us. Our eyes are opened so that we see clearly. Our ears are unstopped so that we have been able to distinctly hear the words which you have spoken. For all these favors we thank the Great Spirit and him only.

Brother! This council fire was kindled by you. It was at your request that we came together at this time. We have listened with attention to what you have said. You have requested us to speak our minds freely. This gives us great joy, for we now consider that we stand upright before you, and can speak what we think. All have heard your voice and all speak to you as one man. Our minds are agreed.

Brother! You say that you want an answer to your talk before you leave this place. It is right that you should have one, as you are a great distance from home, and we do not wish to detain you. But we will first look back a little, and tell you what our fathers have told us, and what we have heard from the white people.

Brother! Listen to what we say. There was a time when our forefathers owned this great island (meaning the continent of North America—a common belief among the Indians). Their seats extended from the rising to the setting of the sun. The Great Spirit had made it for the use of Indians. He had created the buffalo, the deer, and other animals for food. He made the bear and the deer, and their skins served us for clothing. He had scattered them over the country, and had taught us how to take them. He had caused the earth to produce corn for bread. All this he had done for his red children because he loved them.

44

If we had any disputes about hunting grounds, they were generally settled without the shedding of much blood. But an evil day came upon us. Your forefathers crossed the great waters and landed on this island. Their numbers were small. They found friends and not enemies. They told us they had fled from their own country for fear of wicked men, and had come here to enjoy their religion. They asked for a small seat. We took pity on them, granted their request and they sat down amongst us. We gave them corn and meat. They gave us poison (spiritous liquor) in return. The white people had now found our country. Tidings were carried back and more came amongst us. Yet we did not fear them. We took them to be friends. They called us brothers. We believed them and gave them a large seat. At length their numbers had greatly increased. They wanted more land. They wanted our country. Our eyes were opened, and our minds became uneasy. Wars took place. Indians were hired to fight against Indians, and many of our people were destroyed. They also brought strong liquors among us. It was strong and powerful and has slain thousands.

Brother! Our seats were once large, and yours were very small. You have now become a great people, and we have scarcely a place left to spread our blankets. You have got our country, but you are not satisfied. You want to force your religion upon us.

Brother! Continue to listen. You say that you are sent to instruct us how to worship the Great Spirit agreeably to his mind; and if we do not take hold of the religion which you white people teach we shall be unhappy hereafter. You say that you are right, and we are lost. How do you know this to be true? We understand that your religion is written in a book. If it was intended for us as well as for you, why has not the Great Spirit given it to us; and not only to us, but why did he not give to our forefathers the knowledge of that book, with the means of under-

45

standing it rightly? We only know what you tell us about it. How shall we know when to believe, being so often deceived by the white people?

Brother! You say there is but one way to worship and serve the Great Spirit. If there is but one religion, why do you white people differ so much about it? Why not all agree, as you can all read the book?

Brother! We do not understand these things. We are told that your religion was given to your forefathers and has been handed down, father to son. We also have a religion which was given to our forefathers, and has been handed down to us, their children. We worship that way. It teaches us to be thankful for all the favors we received, to love each other, and to be united. We never quarrel about religion.

Brother! The Great Spirit has made us all. But he has made a great difference between his white and red children. He has given us a different complexion and different customs. To you he has given the arts; to these he has not opened our eyes. We know these things to be true. Since he has made so great a difference between us in other things, why may not we conclude that he has given us a different religion, according to our understanding? The Great Spirit does right. He knows what is best for his children. We are satisfied.

Brother! We do not wish to destroy your religion, or to take it from you. We only want to enjoy our own.

Brother! You say you have not come to get our land or our money, but to enlighten our minds. I will now tell you that I have been at your meetings and saw you collecting money from the meeting. I cannot tell what this money was intended for, but suppose it was for your minister; and if we should conform to your way of thinking, perhaps you may want some from us.

Brother! We are told that you have been preaching to the white people in this place. These people are our neighbors. We are acquainted with them. We will wait a little while, and see what effect your preaching has upon them. If we find it does them good and makes them honest and less disposed to cheat Indians, we will then consider again what you have said.

Brother! You have now heard our answer to your talk, and this is all we have to say at present. As we are going to part, we will come and take you by the hand, and hope the Great Spirit will protect you on your journey, and return you safe to your friends.

47

Joseph Brant, Mohawk, born 1742; died November 24, 1807.

Joseph Brant

JOSEPH BRANT, in historical writing often referred to as Captain Brant (sometimes spelled Brandt), was a principal actor in Indian history in early day America. Brant engraved the name Mohawk on the face of American history for all time. He was a gifted speaker, a masterful leader, and at home in any environment. He was able to carry on negotiations with the British, with whom he sided against the colonies, and also to deal with the young American republic.

The fighting of the Six Nations, which the Mohawks in effect led, was a severe threat to the quiet and tranquility of the settlements, and at times threatened the very existence of the colonies.

Brant was born in 1742, and had followed a war party when he was only thirteen years old. He was a skilled military tactician. He died Nov. 24, 1807.

Brant knew that George Washington had worked to get help from the French in the War of Independence from Britain. He determined to reverse the tables, and secured help from the British in his fight on the colonists.

Captain Brant helped to translate various religious works into the Mohawk language. He was a guest of President Washington after peace had been made with the Six Nations, which included the Mohawk, Oneida, Onondaga, Cayuga, Seneca, and Tuscarora tribes.

The talk given here was made at a council held in an Onondaga village on Buffalo Creek, on April 21, 1794.

"We Have Borne Everything Patiently for This Long Time"

Brothers: You, of the United States, listen to what we are going to say to you; you, likewise, the King.

Brothers: We are very happy to see you, Colonel Butler and General Chapin, sitting side by side, with the intent of hearing what we have to say. We wish to do no business but what is done open and above-board.

Brother: You, of the United States, make your mind easy, on account of the long time your President's speech has been under our consideration; when we received it, we told you it was a business of importance, and required some time to be considered of.

Brother: The answer you have brought us is not according to what we expected, which was the reason for our long delay; the business would have been done with expedition, had the United States agreed to our proposals. We would then have collected our associates, and repaired to Venango, the place you proposed for meeting us.

Brother: It is not now in our power to accept your invitation; provided we were to go, you would conduct the business, as you might think proper; this has been the case at all the treaties held, from time to time, by your commissioners.

Brother: At the first treaty, after the conclusion of the war between you and Great Britain, at Fort Stanwix, your commissioners conducted the business as it to them seemed best; they pointed out a line of division, and then confirmed it; after this, they held out that our country was ceded to them by the King; this confused the chiefs who attended there, and prevented them from making any reply to the contrary; still holding out, if we did not consent to it, their warriors were at their back, and that we would get no further protection from Great Britain.

This has ever been held out to us, by the commissioners from Congress; at all the treaties held with us since the peace, at Fort McIntosh, at Rocky River, and every other meeting held, the idea was still the same.

Brother: This has been the case from time to time. Peace has not taken place, because you have held up these ideas, owing to which much mischief has been done to the Southward.

Brother: We, the Six Nations, have been exerting ourselves to keep peace since the conclusion of the war; we think it would be best for both parties; we advised the confederate nations to request a meeting, about half way between us and the United States, in order that such steps might be taken as would bring about a peace; this request was made, and Congress appointed commissioners to meet us at Muskingum, which we agreed to, a boundary line was then proposed by us, and refused by Governor St. Clair, one of your commissioners. The Wyandots, a few Delawares, and some others, met the commissioners, though not authorized, and confirmed the lines of what was not their property, but a common to all nations.

Brothers: The idea we all held out at our council, at Lower Sandusky, held for the purpose of forming our confederacy, and to adopt measures that would be for the general welfare of our Indian nations, or people of our color; owing to those steps taken by us, the United States held out, that when we went to the Westward to transact our private business, that we went with an intention of taking an active part in the troubles subsisting between them and our Western brethren; this never has been the case. We have ever wished for the friendship of the United States.

Brother: We think you must be fully convinced, from our perseverance last summer, as your commissioners saw, that we were anxious for a peace between us. The exertions that we, the Six Nations, have made towards the accomplishing this desirable end, is the cause of the Western nations being somewhat dubious as to our sincerity. After we knew their doubts, we still persevered; and, last fall, we pointed out methods to be taken, and sent them, by you, to Congress; this we certainly expected would have proved satisfactory to the United States; in that case we should have more than ever exerted ourselves, in order that the offers we made should be confirmed by our confederacy, and by them strictly adhered to.

Brother: Our proposals have not met with the success from Congress that we expected; this still leaves us in a similar situation to what we were when we first entered on the business.

Brother: You must recollect the number of chiefs who have, at divers times, waited on Congress; they have pointed out the means to be taken, and held out the same language, uniformly, at one time as another; that was, if you would withdraw your claim to the boundary line, and lands within the line, as offered by us; had this been done, peace would have taken place; and, unless this still be done, we see no other method of accomplishing it.

Brother: We have borne everything patiently for this long time past; we have done everything we could consistently do with the welfare of our nations in general—notwithstanding the many advantages that have been taken of us, by individuals making purchases from us, the Six Nations, whose fraudulent conduct towards us Congress never has taken notice of, nor in any wise seen us rectified, nor made our minds easy. This is the case to the present day; our patience is now entirely worn out; you see the difficulties we labor under, so that we cannot at present rise from our seats and attend your council at Venango, agreeable to your invitation. The boundary line we pointed out, we think is a just one, although the United States claim lands west of that line; the trifle that has been paid by the United States can be no object in comparison to what a peace would be.

Brother: We are of the same opinion with the people of the United States; you consider yourselves as independent people; we, as the original inhabitants of this country, and sovereigns of the soil, look upon ourselves as equally independent, and free as any other nation or nations. This country was given to us by the Great Spirit above; we wish to enjoy it, and have our passage along the lake, within the line we have pointed out.

Brother: The great exertions we have made, for this number of years, to accomplish a peace, and have not been able to obtain it; our patience, as we have already observed, is exhausted, and we are discouraged from persevering any longer. We, therefore, throw ourselves under the protection of the Great Spirit above, who, we hope, will order all things for the best. We have told you our patience is worn out; but not so far, but that we wish for peace, and, whenever we hear that pleasing sound, we shall pay attention to it.

Little Turtle, Miami, born about 1747; died July 14, 1812. From an early portrait by Stuart.

Little Turtle

LITTLE TURTLE was born in a village on the Eel River, about 1747. His father was a chieftain of the Miamis, and his mother was a Mohican. Little Turtle became the war chief of the Miamis at an early age. He was rather short in stature, but well built, with symmetrical form. He had a prominent forehead, heavy eyebrows, keen black eyes, and a large chin.

Little Turtle possessed a remarkable mind, and was for years the leading member of the Miamis. He was unsurpassed for bravery and his intelligence was exceeded by no one else of his race. He lost no opportunity to gain new information and knowledge, and he was interested in just about any subject or object that came to his attention. In later life he used his influence to encourage his people to be peaceful, sober, and industrious.

In .1797 Little Turtle visited Philadelphia, and while there had his portrait painted at the direction of President George Washington. This portrait, done by the famous artist Gilbert Charles Stuart, was later destroyed. Little Turtle had embarrassed President Washington by a series of defeats of the army forces. He was a war leader equal or superior to any the government could put in the field.

Little Turtle was one of the signers of the Treaty of Greenville (Ohio) on August 3, 1795. He had also signed many other treaties in behalf of the Miamis. After signing the Greenville Treaty, Little Turtle remained a faithful friend of the United States, and was much loved and respected by all who knew him.

One early writer said he was "the bravest among the brave, and wisest among the wise of the Indians of the Northwest of his day— leading an army of braves to sure victory one hour—cutting and slashing, as with the ferocity of a tiger, at one moment—and as passive and gentle as a child the next. Ever may his gentler and better deeds be perpetuated by the American people."

Little Turtle, in pressing his claim of title of land around the Great Lakes, said that his ancestors had built the first fire where Detroit was established.

Little Turtle died July 14, 1812, at his lodge, a short distance from the junction of the St. Joseph and the St. Mary rivers. He had suffered for some time from gout, and had moved from the Eel River area to near Fort Wayne, where he sought relief from the U.S. Army surgeon.

The following speech by Little Turtle was made at the Treaty of Greenville (Ohio), the sessions of which began on June 16 and ended August 10, 1795. Little Turtle made this speech on Wednesday, July 29, and it became a part of the report President George Washington sent to the Fourth Congress, First Session, under date of December 9, 1795.

General Anthony Wayne represented the government and conducted the council. The treaty was signed August 7. Representatives of the Wyandottes, Delawares, Shawnees, Ottawas, Chippewas, Potawatomis, Miamis, Eel Rivers, Weas, Kickapoos, Piankeshaws, and Kaskaskias participated and were signatories to the pact.

Little Turtle is speaking of the various conditions in the treaty.

"Brothers, These People Never Told Us They Wished to Purchase Our Lands from Us"

Elder Brother, and all you present: I am going to say a few words, in the name of the Pottawatamies, Weas and Kickapoos. It is well known to you all, that people are appointed on those occasions, to speak the sentiments of others; therefore am I appointed for those three nations.

Elder Brother: You told your younger brothers, when we first assembled, that peace was your object; you swore your interpreters before us, to the faithful discharge of their duty, and told them the Great Spirit would punish them, did they not perform it. You told us, that it was not you, but the President of the Fifteen Fires of the United States, who spoke to us; that,

56

whatever he should say, should be firm and lasting; that it was impossible he should say what was not true. Rest assured, that your younger brothers, the Miamis, Ottawas, Chippewas, Pottawatamies, Shawnees, Weas, Kickapoos, Piankeshaws, and Kaskaskias, are well pleased with your words, and are persuaded of their sincerity. You have told us to consider of the boundaries you showed us; your younger brothers have done so, and now proceed to give you their answer.

Elder Brother: Your younger brothers do not wish to hide their sentiments from you. I wish to be the same with those of the Wyandottes and Delawares; you have told us that most of the reservations you proposed to us belonged to our fathers, the French and the British. Permit your younger brothers to make a few observations on this subject.

Elder Brother: We wish you to listen with attention to our words. You have told your younger brothers that the British imposed falsehoods on us when they said the United States wished to take our lands from us, and that the United States had no such designs. You pointed out to us the boundary line, which crossed a little below Loromie's Store and struck Fort Recovery and run from thence to the Ohio, opposite the mouth of the Kentucky river.

Elder Brother: You have told us to speak our minds freely, and we now do it. This line takes in the greater and best part of your brothers' hunting ground. Therefore, your younger brothers are of opinion you take too much of their lands away and confine the hunting of our young men within the limits too contracted. Your brothers, the Miamis, the proprietors of those lands, and all your younger brothers present, wish you to run the lines as you mentioned to Fort Recovery and to continue it along the road; from thence to Fort Hamilton, on the great Miami River. This is what your brothers request you to do, and

57

you may rest assured of the free navigation of that river, from thence to its mouth, forever.

Brother: Here is the road we wish to be the boundary between us. What lies to the east we wish to be yours; that to the west, we would desire to be ours.

Elder Brother: In speaking of the reservations, you say they are designed for the same purpose as those for which our fathers, the French and English, occupied them. Your younger brothers now wish to make some observations on them.

Elder Brother: Listen to me with attention. You told us you discovered on the Great Miami traces of an old fort. It was not a French fort, brother; it was a fort built by me. You perceived another at Loromies. 'Tis true a Frenchman once lived there for a year or two. The Miami villages were occupied as you remarked, but it was unknown to your younger brothers until you told them that we had sold the land there to the French or English. I was much surprised to hear you say that it was my forefathers had set the example to other Indians in selling their lands. I will inform you in what manner the French and English occupied those places.

Elder Brother: These people were seen by our forefathers first at Detroit. Afterwards we saw them at the Miami village—that glorious gate, which your younger brothers had the happiness to own, and through which all the good words of our chiefs had to pass, from the north to the south, and from the east to the west. Brothers, these people never told us they wished to purchase our lands from us.

Elder Brother: I now give you the true sentiment of your younger brothers the Miamis, with respect to the reservation at the Miami villages. We thank you for kindly contracting the limits you at first proposed. We wish you to take this six miles square on the side of the river where your fort now stands, as your younger brothers wish to inhabit that beloved spot again.

You shall cut hay for your cattle wherever you please, and you shall never require in vain the assistance of your younger brothers at that place.

Elder Brother: The next place you pointed to was the Little River, and said you wanted two miles square at that place. This is a request that our fathers, the French or British, never made us. It was always ours. This carrying place has heretofore proved in a great degree the subsistence of your younger brothers. That place has brought us in the course of one day the amount of one hundred dollars. Let us both own this place and enjoy in common the advantages it affords. You told us at Chicago the French possessed a fort. We have never heard of it. We thank you for the trade you promised to open in our country, and permit us to remark that we wish our former traders may be continued and mixed with yours.

Elder Brother: On the subject of hostages, I have only to observe that I trust all my brothers present are of my opinion with regard to peace and our future happiness. I expect to be with you every day when you settle on your reservations, and it will be impossible for me or my people to withhold from you a single prisoner. Therefore, we don't know why any of us should remain here. These are the sentiments of your younger brothers present, on these particulars.

Tecumseh, Shawnee, born 1768; died October 5, 1813. Illustration from a pencil sketch made in 1808, to which the cap, medal, and uniform were added.

Tecumseh

TECUMSEH is outstanding among Indian orators and warriors. His Shawnees attempted to crystallize opposition to the encroachment of the whites by forming a coalition among the Wyandottes, Delawares, some of the Algonquins, the Chippewas, Nanticokes, Creeks, and Cherokees. At the time of the greatest activity the Shawnees lived with the Delawares.

Tecumseh is reported to have had twin brothers. One writer says the mother gave birth to three sons about 1770, the most noted being Tecumseh (meaning cougar crouching for his prey); the others were Laulewasikau or Ellskwatawa (an open door), who achieved fame as The Prophet, and Rumskaka or Kumskaukau, who did little to attract attention during his life.

Tecumseh made long horseback trips over most of the South, trying to enlist the tribes in his cause. He argued that the United States government had no right to buy land from a single tribe, because the land belonged in common to all tribes. Tecumseh went into Canada several times, and even crossed westward over the Mississippi in his journeys. He lived in a settlement on the Wabash River near the mouth of the Tippecanoe.

At the beginning of the War of 1812, Tecumseh went to Canada, where he was highly esteemed. The British commissioned him a brigadier general in their forces.

Tecumseh was killed in battle on the Thames River, near Chatham, Ontario, on October 5, 1813.

In the spring of 1811, Tecumseh called for a council with the tribes in the southern part of the country. Accompanied by a party of some thirty braves, he appeared at a gathering of the Choctaws and Chickasaws, and made a plea for them to join in a common effort against the whites. Tecumseh eloquently made an appeal for unity, and it was evident that he found some of the Choctaws and Chickasaws sympathetic to his appeal.

However, he had not anticipated the hold that Pushmataha, chief of the Choctaws, had upon his people. Pushmataha spoke before the same council, and his answer to the speech of Tecumseh is also given in this collection. In spite of Tecumseh's power as an orator, it seems that on this occasion Pushmataha bested him and was able to prevent the Choctaws and Chickasaws from joining in what later became the War of 1812.

~ "Sleep Not Longer, O Choctaws and Chickasaws"

In view of questions of vast importance, have we met together in solemn council tonight. Nor should we here debate whether we have been wronged and injured, but by what measures we should avenge ourselves; for our merciless oppressors, having long since planned out their proceedings, are not about to make, but have and are still making attacks upon our race who have as yet come to no resolution. Nor are we ignorant by what steps, and by what gradual advances, the whites break in upon our neighbors. Imagining themselves to be still undiscovered, they show themselves the less audacious because you are insensible. The whites are already nearly a match for us all united, and too strong for any one tribe alone to resist; so that unless we support one another with our collective and united forces; unless every tribe unanimously combines to give check to the ambition and avarice of the whites, they will soon conquer us apart and disunited, and we will be driven away from our native country and scattered as autumnal leaves before the wind.

But have we not courage enough remaining to defend our country and maintain our ancient independence? Will we calmly suffer the white intruders and tyrants to enslave us? Shall it be said of our race that we knew not how to extricate ourselves from the three most dreadful calamities—folly, inactivity and cowardice? But what need is there to speak of the past? It speaks for itself and asks, Where today is the Pequod? Where the Narragansetts, the Mohawks, Pocanokets, and many other once powerful tribes of our race? They have vanished before the avarice and oppression of the white men, as snow before a summer sun. In the vain hope of alone defending their ancient possessions, they have fallen in the wars with the white men. Look abroad over their once beautiful country, and what see you now? Naught but the ravages of the pale face destroyers meet our eyes. So it will be with you Choctaws and Chickasaws! Soon your mighty forest trees, under the shade of whose wide spreading branches you have played in infancy, sported in boyhood, and now rest your wearied limbs after the fatigue of the chase, will be cut down to fence in the land which the white intruders dare to call their own. Soon their broad roads will pass over the grave of your fathers, and the place of their rest will be blotted out forever. The annihilation of our race is at hand unless we unite in one common cause against the common foe. Think not, brave Choctaws and Chickasaws, that you can remain passive and indifferent to the common danger, and thus escape the common fate. Your people, too, will soon be as falling leaves and scattering clouds before their blighting breath. You, too, will be driven away from your native land and ancient domains as leaves are driven before the wintry storms.

Sleep not longer, O Choctaws and Chickasaws, in false security and delusive hopes. Our broad domains are fast escaping from our grasp. Every year our white intruders become more greedy, exacting, oppressive and overbearing. Every year contentions spring up between them and our people and when blood is shed we have to make atonement whether right or wrong, at the cost of the lives of our greatest chiefs, and the yielding up of large tracts of our lands. Before the palefaces came among us, we enjoyed the happiness of unbounded freedom, and were acquainted with neither riches, wants nor oppression. How is it now? Wants and oppression are our lot; for are we not controlled in everything, and dare we move without asking, by your leave? Are we not being stripped day by day of the little that remains of our ancient liberty? Do they not even kick and strike us as they do their black-faces? How long will it be before they will tie us to a post and whip us, and make us work for them in their corn fields as they do them? Shall we wait for that moment or shall we die fighting before submitting to such ignominy?

Have we not for years had before our eyes a sample of their designs, and are they not sufficient harbingers of their future determinations? Will we not soon be driven from our respective countries and the graves of our ancestors? Will not the bones of our dead be plowed up, and their graves be turned into fields? Shall we calmly wait until they become so numerous that we will no longer be able to resist oppression? Will we wait to be destroyed in our turn, without making an effort worthy of our race? Shall we give up our homes, our country, bequeathed to us by the Great Spirit, the graves of our dead, and everything that is dear and sacred to us, without a struggle? I know you will cry with me: Never! Never! Then let us by unity of action destroy them all, which we now can do, or drive them back whence they came. War or extermination is now our only choice. Which do you choose? I know your answer. Therefore, I now call on you, brave Choctaws and Chickasaws, to assist in the just cause of liberating our race from the grasp of our faithless invaders and heartless oppressors. The white usurpation in our common country must be stopped, or we, its rightful owners, be forever destroyed and wiped out as a race of people. I am now at the head of many warriors backed by the strong arm of English soldiers. Choctaws and Chickasaws, you have too long borne with grievous usurpation inflicted by the arrogant Americans. Be no longer their dupes. If there be one here tonight who believes that his rights will not sooner or later be taken from him by the avaricious American pale faces, his ignorance ought to excite pity, for he knows little of the character of our common foe.

And if there be one among you mad enough to undervalue the growing power of the white race among us, let him tremble in considering the fearful woes he will bring down upon our entire race, if by his criminal indifference he assists the designs of our common enemy against our common country. Then listen to the voice of duty, of honor, of nature and of your endangered country. Let us form one body, one heart, and defend to the last warrior our country, our homes, our liberty, and the graves of our fathers.

Choctaws and Chickasaws, you are among the few of our race who sit indolently at ease. You have indeed enjoyed the reputation of being brave, but will you be indebted for it more from report than fact? Will you let the whites encroach upon your domains even to your very door before you will assert your rights in resistance? Let no one in this council imagine that I speak more from malice against the pale face Americans than just grounds of complaint. Complaint is just toward friends who have failed in their duty; accusation is against enemies guilty of injustice. And surely, if any people ever had, we have good and just reasons to believe we have ample grounds to accuse the Americans of injustice; especially when such great acts of injustice have been committed by them upon our race, of which they seem to have no manner of regard, or even to reflect. They are a people fond of innovations, quick to contrive and quick to put their schemes into effectual execution no matter how great the wrong and injury to us; while we are content to preserve what we already have. Their designs are to enlarge their possessions by taking yours in turn; and will you, can you longer dally, O Choctaws and Chickasaws?

Do you imagine that that people will not continue longest in the enjoyment of peace who timely prepare to vindicate themselves, and manifest a determined resolution to do themselves right whenever they are wronged? Far otherwise. Then haste to the relief of our common cause, as by consanguinity of blood you are bound; lest the day be not far distant when you will be left single-handed and alone to the cruel mercy of our most inveterate foe.

Two years after Tecumseh made his appeal to the Choctaws and the Chickasaws to join in a move to stop the advance of the whites, he had occasion to address the British commander in the northern part of the country. The naval battle to which he refers is that in which Commodore Oliver Hazard Perry defeated the British ships on Lake Erie, on September 10, 1813, and broke British sea power on the inland lakes. Perry reported the destruction of two ships, two brigs, one schooner, and a sloop. Tecumseh was concerned because he was aware that the battle had been fought but he could not find out who had been successful. At the time of the speech, the British were busily preparing to withdraw from the area.

This speech was delivered to General Proctor, the British commander, who was directing the work of evacuating the base at Malden.

"Father, Listen! The Americans Have Not Yet Defeated Us by Land"

Father, listen to your children! You have them now all before you.

The war before this, our British father gave the hatchet to his red children, when our old chiefs were alive. They are now dead. In the war, our father was thrown on his back by the Americans, and our father took them by the hand without our knowledge; and we are afraid that our father will do so again this time.

Summer before last, when I came forward with my red brethren, and was ready to take up the hatchet in favor of our British father, we were told not to be in a hurry, that he had not yet determined to fight the Americans.

Listen! When war was declared, our father stood up and gave us the tomahawk and told us that he was then ready to strike the Americans; that he wanted our assistance; and that he would certainly get our lands back, which the Americans had taken from us.

Listen! You told us, at that time, to bring forward our families to this place; and we did so; and you promised to take care of them, and they should want for nothing, while the men would go out and fight the enemy; that we need not trouble ourselves about the enemy's garrisons; that we knew nothing about them, and that our father would attend to that part of the business. You also told your red children that you would take good care of your garrison here, which made our hearts glad.

Listen! When we were last at the Rapids it is true we gave you little assistance. It is hard to fight people who live like groundhogs.

Father, listen! Our fleet has gone out. We know they have fought. We have heard the great guns, but we know nothing of what has happened to our father with that arm. Our ships have gone one way, and we are much astonished to see our father tying up everything and preparing to run away the other, without letting his red children know what his intentions are. You always told us to remain here and take care of our lands. It made our hearts glad to hear that was your wish. Our great father, the king, is the head, and you represent him. You always told us that you would never draw your foot off British ground; but now, father, we see you are drawing back, and we are sorry to see our father doing so without seeing the enemy. We must compare our father's conduct to a fat dog, that carries its tail upon its back, but when afrighted, it drops it between its legs and runs off.

Father, listen! The Americans have not yet defeated us by

land. Neither are we sure that they have done so by water. We therefore wish to remain here and fight our enemy, should they make their appearance. If they defeat us, we will then retreat with our father.

At the battle of the Rapids, last war, the Americans certainly defeated us, and when we retreated to our father's fort at that place the gates were shut against us. We were afraid that it would now be the case; but instead of that, we now see our British father preparing to march out of his garrison.

Father! You have got the arms and ammunition which our great father sent for his red children. If you have an idea of going away, give them to us, and you may go and welcome for us. Our lives are in the hands of the Great Spirit. We are determined to defend our lands, and if it be his will, we wish to leave our bones upon them.

Pushmataha, Choctaw, born about 1764; died December 24, 1824.

Pushmataha

PUSHMATAHA, one of the most active leaders of the Choctaw Indians, was born in what is now Noxubee County, Mississippi, in 1764. Little is known of his origin, but this worried Pushmataha not a bit. He is reported to have said: "I had no father. I had no mother. The lightning rent the living oak, and Pushmataha sprang forth."

"Push," as he was referred to by some of his contemporaries, was dedicated to the cause of the Choctaws, who were always friendly to the whites. Pushmataha with his Choctaws sided with the whites in their fight against the warlike tribes, and he earned the title of "The Indian General" because of the discipline he enforced among his warriors. He opposed the efforts of Tecumseh in trying to organize all Indians into military action against the whites.

Pushmataha made a number of trips to Washington and, over the years, was familiar with several presidents. He played a conspicuous role in the inauguration processional of President Andrew Jackson.

President James Monroe and Secretary of War John Calhoun met their match with Pushmataha as a negotiator. His continuous efforts to help the Choctaws caused the tribe to hold his memory dear.

Pushmataha went to Washington in 1824 on still another mission. Exposure to severe weather caused him to fall ill and he died there December 24, 1824, aged about sixty years. He was buried in the old Congressional Cemetery, where a military salute was fired after the mile-long funeral procession ended at the grave.

To the last, Pushmataha was faithful to his people.

The speech given here was made by Pushmatahta following one in which Tecumseh was trying to get the Choctaws to join his rebellion. Read the reasoning of Pushmataha, as he spoke in 1811.

"We Do Not Take Up the Warpath Without a Just Cause and Honest Purpose"

Attention, my good red warriors! Hear ye my brief remarks.

The great Shawnee orator has portrayed in vivid picture the wrongs inflicted on his and other tribes by the ravages of the paleface. The candor and fervor of his eloquent appeal breathe the conviction of truth and sincerity, and, as kindred tribes, naturally we sympathize with the misfortunes of his people. I do not come before you in any disputation either for or against these charges. It is not my purpose to contradict any of these allegations against the white man, but neither am I here to indulge in any indiscreet denunciation of him which might bring down upon my people unnecessary difficulty and embarrassment.

The distinguished Shawnee sums up his eloquent appeal to us with this direct question:

"Will you sit idly by, supinely awaiting complete and abject submission, or will you die fighting beside your brethren, the Shawnees, rather than submit to such ignominy?"

These are plain words and it is well they have been spoken, for they bring the issue squarely before us. Mistake not, this language means war. And war with whom, pray? War with some band of marauders who have committed there depredations against the Shawnees? War with some alien host seeking the destruction of the Choctaws and Chickasaws? Nay, my fellow tribesmen. None of these are the enemy we will be called on to meet. If we take up arms against the Americans we must of necessity meet in deadly combat our daily neighbors and associates in this part of the country near our homes.

If Tecumseh's words be true, and we doubt them not, then the Shawnee's experience with the whites has not been the same as that of the Choctaws. These white Americans buy our skins, our corn, our cotton, our surplus game, our baskets, and other wares, and they give us in fair exchange their cloth, their guns, their tools, implements, and other things which the Choctaws need but do not make. It is true we have befriended them, but who will deny that these acts of friendship have been abundantly reciprocated? They have given us cotton gins, which simplify the spinning and sale of our cotton; they have encouraged and helped us in the production of our crops; they have taken many of our wives into their homes to teach them useful things, and pay them for their work while learning; they teach our children to read and write from their books. You all remember the dreadful epidemic visited upon us last winter. During its darkest hours these neighbors whom we are now urged to attack responded generously to our needs. They doctored our sick; they clothed our suffering; they fed our hungry; and where is the Choctaw or Chickasaw delegation who has ever gone to St. Stephens with a worthy cause and been sent away empty handed? So, in marked contrast with the experiences of the Shawnees, it will be seen that the whites and Indians in this section are living on friendly and mutually beneficial terms.

Forget not, O Choctaws and Chickasaws, that we are bound in peace to the Great White Father at Washington by a sacred treaty and the Great Spirit will punish those who break their word. The Great White Father has never violated that treaty and the Choctaws have never been driven to the necessity of taking up the tomahawk against him or his children. Therefore the question before us tonight is not the avenging of any wrongs perpetrated against us by the whites, for the Choctaws and Chickasaws have no such cause, either real or imaginary, but rather it is a question of carrying on that record of fidelity and justice for which our forefathers ever proudly stood, and doing that which is best calculated to promote the welfare of our own people. Yea, my fellow tribesmen, we are a just people. We do not take up the warpath without a just cause and honest purpose. Have we that just cause against our white neighbors, who have taken nothing from us except by fair bargain and exchange? Is this a just recompense for their assistance to us in our agricultural and other pursuits? Is this to be their gracious reward for teaching our children from their books? Shall this be considered the Choctaws' compensation for feeding our hungry, clothing our needy, and administering to our sick? Have we, O Choctaws and Chickasaws, descended to the low estate of ruthlessly breaking the faith of a sacred treaty? Shall our forefathers look back from the happy hunting grounds only to see their unbroken record for justice, gratitude, and fidelity thus rudely repudiated and abruptly abandoned by an unworthy offspring?

We Choctaws and Chickasaws are a peaceful people, making our subsistence by honest toil; but mistake not, my Shawnee brethren, we are not afraid of war. Neither are we strangers to war, as those who have undertaken to encroach upon our rights in the past may abundantly testify. We are thoroughly familiar with war in all its details and we know full well all its horrible consequences. It is unnecessary for me to remind you, O Choctaws and Chickasaws, veteran braves of many fierce conflicts in the past, that war is an awful thing. If we go into this war against the Americans, we must be prepared to accept its inevitable results. Not only will it foretoken deadly conflict with neighbors and death to warriors, but it will mean suffering for our women, hunger and starvation for our children, grief for our loved ones, and devastation of our beloved homes. Notwithstanding these difficulties, if the cause be just, we should not hesitate to defend our rights to the last man, but before that fatal step is irrevocably taken, it is well that we fully understand and seriously consider the full portent and consequences of the act.

Hear me, O Choctaws and Chickasaws, for I speak truly for your welfare. It is not the province of your chiefs to settle these

74

important questions. As a people, it is your prerogative to have either peace or war, and as one of your chiefs, it is mine simply to counsel and advise. Therefore, let me admonish you that this critical period is no time to cast aside your wits and let blind impulse sway; be not driven like dumb brutes by the frenzied harangue of this wonderful Shawnee orator; let your good judgment rule and ponder seriously before breaking bonds that have served you well and ere you change conditions which have brought peace and happiness to your wives, your sisters, and your children. I would not undertake to dictate the course of one single Choctaw warrior. Permit me to speak for the moment, not as your chief but as a Choctaw warrior, weighing this question beside you. As such I shall exercise my calm, deliberate judgment in behalf of those most dear to me and dependent on me, and I shall not suffer my reason to be swept away by this eloquent recital of alleged wrongs which I know naught of. I deplore this war, I earnestly hope it may be averted, but if it be forced upon us I shall take my stand with those who have stood by my people in the past and will be found fighting beside our good friends of St. Stephens and surrounding country. I have finished. I call on all Choctaws and Chickasaws indorsing my sentiments to cast their tomahawks on this side of the council fire with me.

> (The warriors overwhelmingly supported Pushmataha, which caused Tecumseh to declare that Pushmataha was a coward and that the Choctaws and Chickasaw warriors were squaws. As rebuttal, Pushmataha made another statement, speaking as follows.)

Halt, Tecumseh! Listen to me. You have come here, as you have often gone elsewhere, with a purpose to involve peaceful people in unnecessary trouble with their neighbors. Our people have had no undue friction with the whites. Why? Because we have had no leaders stirring up strife to serve their selfish, personal ambitions. You heard me say that our people are a peaceful people. They make their way, not by ravages upon their neighbors but by honest toil. In that regard they have nothing in common with you. I know your history well. You are a disturber. You have ever been a trouble maker. When you have found yourself unable to pick a quarrel with the white man, you have stirred up strife between different tribes of your own race. Not only that, you are a monarch and unyielding tyrant within your own domain; every Shawnee man, woman, and child must bow in humble submission to your imperious will. The Choctaws and Chickasaws have no monarchs. Their chieftains do not undertake the mastery of their people, but rather are they the people's servants, elected to serve the will of the majority. The majority has spoken on this question and it has spoken against your contention. Their decision has therefore become the law of the Choctaws and Chickasaws and Pushmataha will see that the will of the majority so recently expressed is rigidly carried out to the letter.

If, after this decision, any Choctaw should be so foolish as to follow your imprudent advice and enlist to fight against the Americans, thereby abandoning his own people and turning against the decision of his own council, Pushmataha will see that proper punishment is meted out to him, which is death. You have made your choice; you have elected to fight with the British. The Americans have been our friends and we shall stand by them. We will furnish you safe conduct to the boundaries of this nation as properly befits the dignity of your office. Farewell, Tecumseh. You will see Pushmataha no more until we meet on the fateful warpath.

Petalesharo, Pawnee, born about 1797; died 1874.

Petalesharo

PETALESHARO was a handsome principal chief of the Pawnee Indians. He succeeded his father as chief and served his people in a distinguished career. Born in 1797, Petalesharo participated in events which have added much color to his reputation. There were several Pawnee chiefs who bore the same name of Petalesharo during this period, and it is sometimes difficult to attribute their deeds to the proper person.

His tribe, the Pawnee Loups or the Skidi Pawnee, were one of the few tribes north of Mexico to practice human sacrifice. Petalesharo daringly rescued an Indian maiden from death at one of the sacrificial ceremonies. His action in rescuing the young woman from death was told in the East on his trip to visit the Great Father and created quite a stir among the citizens, who made him the subject of much attention and approval. Petalesharo was influential in abolishing human sacrifice from the Pawnee ritual.

While in Washington, Petalesharo was a guest of President James Monroe and Secretary of War John Calhoun. His party stayed in Washington from October, 1821, until the following March. He visited Baltimore, New York, and Philadelphia, and attended a New Year's reception at the White House.

Petalesharo died in 1874, after a useful and active life.

The speech given here was delivered at a conference on February 4, 1822, at which President Monroe was one of the participants. President Monroe had urged the chief and his people to follow the way of peace and to be friendly with the people of the United States. The speech is a fine example of reasoning and presentation of Indian points of view.

79

"It Is Too Soon, My Great Father, to Send Those Good Men Among Us"

My Great Father: I have traveled a great distance to see you—I have seen you and my heart rejoices. I have heard your words—they have entered one ear and shall not escape the other, and I will carry them to my people as pure as they came from your mouth.

My Great Father: I am going to speak the truth. The Great Spirit looks down upon us, and I call Him to witness all that may pass between us on this occasion. If I am here now and have seen your people, your houses, your vessels on the big lake, and a great many wonderful things far beyond my comprehension, which appear to have been made by the Great Spirit and placed in your hands. I am indebted to my Father here, who invited me from home, under whose wings I have been protected. Yes, my Great Father, I have traveled with your chief; I have followed him, and trod in his tracks; but there is still another Great Father to whom I am much indebted—it is the Father of us all. Him who made us and placed us on this earth. I feel grateful to the Great Spirit for strengthening my heart for such an undertaking, and for preserving the life which he gave me. The Great Spirit made us all—he made my skin red, and yours white; he placed us on this earth, and intended that we should live differently from each other.

He made the whites to cultivate the earth, and feed on domestic animals; but he made us, red skins, to rove through the uncultivated woods and plains; to feed on wild animals; and to dress with their skins. He also intended that we should go to war—to take scalps—steal horses from and triumph over our enemies—cultivate peace at home, and promote the happiness of each other. I believe there are no people of any colour on this earth who do not believe in the Great Spirit—in rewards, and in punishments. We worship him, but we worship him not as you do. We differ from you in appearance and manners as well as in our customs; and we differ from you in our religion; we have no large houses as you have to worship the Great Spirit in; if we had them today, we should want others tomorrow, for we have not, like you, a fixed habitation—we have no settled home except our villages, where we remain but two moons in twelve. We, like animals, rove through the country, whilst you whites reside between us and heaven; but still, my Great Father, we love the Great Spirit—we acknowledge his supreme power—our peace, our health, and our happiness depend upon him, and our lives belong to him—he made us and he can destroy us.

My Great Father: Some of your good chiefs, as they are called (missionaries), have proposed to send some of their good people among us to change our habits, to make us work and live like the white people. I will not tell a lie—I am going to tell the truth. You love your country—you love your people—you love the manner in which they live, and you think your people brave. I am like you, my Great Father, I love my country—I love my people—I love the manner in which they live, and think myself and warriors brave. Spare me then, Father; let me enjoy my country, and pursue the buffalo, and the beaver, and the other wild animals of our country, and I will trade their skins with your people. I have grown up, and lived thus long without work—I am in hopes you will suffer me to die without it. We have plenty of buffalo, beaver, deer and other wild animals—we have also an abundance of horses—we have everything we want—we have plenty of land, if you will keep your people off of it. My father has a piece on which he lives (Council Bluffs) and we wish him to enjoy it—we have enough without it—but we wish him to live near us to give us good counsel—to keep our ears and eyes open that we may continue to pursue the right road—the road to happiness. He settles all differences between us and the whites,

81

between the red skins themselves—he makes the whites do justice to the red skins, and he makes the red skins do justice to the whites. He saves the effusion of human blood, and restores peace and happiness on the land. You have already sent us a father; it is enough he knows us and we know him—we have confidence in him—we keep our eye constantly upon him, and since we have heard your words, we will listen more attentively to his.

It is too soon, my Great Father, to send those good men among us. We are not starving yet—we wish you to permit us to enjoy the chase until the game of our country is exhausted—until the wild animals become extinct. Let us exhaust our present resources before you make us toil and interrupt our happiness—let me continue to live as I have done, and after I have passed to the Good or Evil Spirit from off the wilderness of my present life, the subsistence of my children may become so precarious as to need and embrace the assistance of those good people.

There was a time when we did not know the whites—our wants were then fewer than they are now. They were always within our control—we had then seen nothing which we could not get. Before our intercourse with the whites (who have caused such a destruction in our game), we could lie down and sleep, and when we awoke we would find the buffalo feeding around our camp—but now we are killing them for their skins, and feeding the wolves with their flesh, to make our children cry over their bones.

Here, my Great Father, is a pipe which I present you, as I am accustomed to present pipes to all the red skins in peace with us. It is filled with such tobacco as we were accustomed to smoke before we knew the white people. It is pleasant, and the spontaneous growth of the most remote parts of our country. I know that the robes, leggins, mockasins, bear claws, etc., are of little value to you, but we wish you to have them deposited and preserved in some conspicuous part of your lodge, so that when we are gone and the sod turned over our bones, if our children should visit this place, as we do now, they may see and recognize with pleasure the deposits of their fathers; and reflect on the times that are past.

Black Hawk, Sac, born 1767; died October 3, 1838.

Black Hawk

BLACK HAWK was untiring in his efforts to get his tribe, the Sauks, to continue their fight against the whites. He had a spellbinding ability by which he could inflame his Indian listeners. Early in life he had proven himself as a warrior. He participated in war parties at age fifteen, and received tribal recognition for his exploits. At seventeen he led a war party. He was very active in all the raiding done by the Sauks. During the War of 1812 he was an active participant on the side of the British.

Black Hawk was born in a village at the mouth of the Rock River, in Illinois, in 1767. He died at his home near Iowaville, on the Des Moines River, on October 3, 1838, at the age of seventy-two.

The first speech quoted here was made in April, 1832, when Black Hawk was attempting to incite the Sauks to take the warpath against the whites. The Sauks had in one of the lodges a white prisoner who heard the whole speech and ceremony, in which the Sauks danced and sang, and finally listened to Black Hawk.

As his efforts to defeat the whites failed, Black Hawk finally surrendered and listened to offers of peace. He was sent to Washington as a prisoner, and had a conference with President Andrew Jackson. The President chided him for bringing on war, and Black Hawk responded: "Sir, you are a man; so am I. But fortune has placed us in different circumstances. Your people are stronger than mine. You can dictate your terms. I am your prisoner, and must submit, but I am still a man, the same as you."

Black Hawk was also sent to Norfolk, Baltimore, Philadelphia, and New York, to impress upon him the strength and greatness of the nation. He finally realized he had come up against an immovable force, and that he could no longer stay the white horde.

*"For More Than a Hundred Winters Our Nation
Was a Powerful, Happy, and United People"*

Head-men, Chiefs, Braves and Warriors of the Sauks: For
more than a hundred winters our nation was a powerful, happy
and united people. The Great Spirit gave to us a territory, seven
hundred miles in length, along the Mississippi, reaching from
Prairie du Chien to the mouth of the Illinois river. This vast
territory was composed of some of the finest and best land for
the home and use of the Indian ever found in this country. The
woods and prairies teemed with buffalo, moose, elk, bear and
deer, with other game suitable to our enjoyment, while its lakes,
rivers, creeks and ponds were alive with the very best kinds of
fish, for our food. The islands in the Mississippi were our gar-
dens, where the Great Spirit caused berries, plums and other
fruits to grow in great abundance, while the soil, when cultivated, produced corn, beans, pumpkins and squash of the finest
quality and largest quantities. Our children were never known
to cry of hunger, and no stranger, red or white, was permitted to
enter our lodges without finding food and rest. Our nation was
respected by all who came in contact with it, for we had the
ability as well as the courage to defend and maintain our rights
of territory, person and property against the world. Then, indeed, was it an honor to be called a Sauk, for that name was a
passport to our people traveling in other territories and among
other nations. But an evil day befell us when we became a
divided nation, and with that division our glory deserted us,
leaving us with the hearts and heels of the rabbit in place of the
courage and strength of the bear.

All this was brought about by the long guns, who now claim
all our territory east of the Mississippi, including Saukenuk, our
ancient village, where all of us were born, raised, lived, hunted,
fished and loved, and near which are our corn lands, which have

yielded abundant harvests for an hundred winters, and where sleep the bones of our sacred dead, and around which cluster our fondest recollections of heroism and noble deeds of charity done by our fathers, who were Sauks, not only in name, but in courage and action. I thank the Great Spirit for making me a Sauk, and the son of a great Sauk chief, and a lineal descendant of Nana-makee, the founder of our nation.

The Great Spirit is the friend and protector of the Sauks, and has accompanied me as your War Chief upon the war-path against our enemies, and has given me skill to direct and you the courage to achieve an hundred victories over our enemies upon the war-path. All this occurred before we became a divided nation. We then had the courage and strength of the bear, but since the division our hearts and heels are like those of the rabbit and fawn. We have neither courage or confidence in our leaders or ourselves, and have fallen a prey to internal jealousies and petty strifes until we are no longer worth of the illustrious name we bear. In a word, we have become subjects of ridicule and bandinage,—"there goes a cowardly Sauk." All this has resulted from the white man's accursed fire-water united with our own tribal quarrels and personal jealousies. The Great Spirit created this country for the use and benefit of his red children, and placed them in full possession of it, and we were happy and contented. Why did he send the palefaces across the great ocean to take it from us? When they landed on our territory they were received as long-absent brothers whom the Great Spirit had returned to us. Food and rest were freely given them by our fathers, who treated them all the more kindly on account of their weak and helpless condition. Had our fathers the desire, they could have crushed the intruders out of existence with the same ease we kill the blood-sucking mosquitoes. Little did our fathers then think they were taking to their bosoms, and warming them to life, a lot of torpid, half-frozen and starving vipers, which in a few winters would fix their deadly fangs upon the very bosoms that had nursed and cared for them when they needed help.

From the day when the palefaces landed upon our shores, they have been robbing us of our inheritance, and slowly, but surely, driving us back, back, back towards the setting sun, burning our villages, destroying our growing crops, ravishing our wives and daughters, beating our papooses with cruel sticks, and brutally murdering our people upon the most flimsy pretenses and trivial causes.

Upon our return to Saukenuk from our winter hunting grounds last spring, we found the palefaces in our lodges, and that they had torn down our fences and were plowing our corn lands and getting ready to plant their corn upon the lands which the Sauks have owned and cultivated for so many winters that our memory cannot go back to them. Nor is this all. They claim to own our lands and lodges by right of purchase from the cowardly and treacherous Quashquamme, nearly thirty winters ago, and drive us away from our lodges and fields with kicks of their cruel boots, accompanied with vile cursing and beating with sticks. When returning from an ill-fated day's hunt, wearied and hungry, with my feet stumbling with the weight of sixty-four winters, I was basely charged by two palefaces of killing their hogs, which I indignantly denied because the charges were false, but they told me I lied, and then they took my gun, powder-horn and bullet-pouch from me by violence, and beat me with a hickory stick until blood ran down my back like drops of falling rain, and my body was so lame and sore for a moon that I could not hunt or fish. They brought their accursed fire-water to our village, making wolves of our braves and warriors, and then when we protested against the sale and destroyed their bad spirits, they came with a multitude on horseback, compelling us to flee across the Mississippi for our lives, and then they burned down our ancient village and turned their horses into our growing corn.

They are now running their plows through our graveyards, turning up the bones and ashes of our sacred dead, whose spirits are calling to us from the land of dreams for vengeance on the despoilers. Will the descendants of Nanamakee and our other illustrious dead stand idly by and suffer this sacrilege to be continued? Have they lost their strength and courage, and become squaws and pappooses? The Great Spirit whispers in my ear, no! Then let us be again united as a nation and at once cross the Mississippi, rekindle our watchfires upon our ancient watch-tower, and send forth the war-whoop of the again united Sauks, and our cousins, the Masquawkees, Pottawattamies, Ottawas, Chippewas, Winnebagoes and Kickapoos, will unite with us in avenging our wrongs upon the white pioneers of Illinois.

When we recross the Mississippi with a strong army, the British Father will send us not only guns, tomahawks, spears, knives and ammunition in abundance, but he will also send us British soldiers to fight our battles for us. Then will the deadly arrow and fatal tomahawk hurtle through the air at the hearts and heads of the pale faced invaders, sending their guilty spirits to the white man's place of endless punishment, and should we, while on the warpath, meet the Pauguk, our departing spirits will be led along that path which is strewn with beautiful flowers, laden with the fragrance of patriotism and heroism, which leads to the land of dreams, whence the spirit of our fathers are beckoning us on, to avenge their wrongs.

Following years of trouble in a time when the whites were pushing ever westward and occupying Indian lands, Black Hawk finally decided to take the warpath again. In the spring of 1832 Black Hawk and his followers crossed to the east side of the Mississippi River, either to raise a corn crop with his people or to attack the whites. He was attacked by troops of the United States and Illinois, and a merciless war resulted. Severe losses were incurred by the Indians, and in an attempt to escape, Black Hawk was captured by two Winnebago Indians, on August 27, 1832.

It is thought that Black Hawk made the following speech when he was turned over to the Indian Agent at Prairie du Chien. This is probably one of the most touching of the recorded Indian speeches.

"Farewell to Black Hawk"

You have taken me prisoner, with all my warriors. I am much grieved; for I expected, if I did not defeat you, to hold out much longer, and give you more trouble before I surrendered. I tried hard to bring you into ambush, but your last general understood Indian fighting. I determined to rush upon you, and fight you face to face. I fought hard, but your guns were well aimed. The bullets flew like birds in the air, and whizzed by our ears like the wind through the trees in winter.

My warriors fell around me; it began to look dismal. I saw my evil day at hand. The sun rose dim on us in the morning, and at night it sank in a dark cloud, and looked like a ball of fire. That was the last sun that shone on Black Hawk. His heart is dead, and no longer beats quick in his bosom. He is now a prisoner to the white men; they will do with him as they wish. But he can stand torture, and is not afraid of death. He is no coward. Black Hawk is an Indian!

He has done nothing for which an Indian ought to be ashamed. He has fought for his countrymen, against the white men who came, year after year, to cheat them and take away their lands. You know the cause of our making war. It is known to all white men. They ought to be ashamed of it. The white men despise the Indians and drive them back from their homes. But the Indians are not deceitful. The white men speak bad of the

Indian, and look at him spitefully. But the Indian does not tell lies. Indians do not steal. An Indian who is as bad as a white man could not live in our nation. He would be put to death and eaten by the wolves.

The white men are bad schoolmasters. They carry false looks and deal in false actions. They smile in the face of the poor Indian, to cheat him; they shake him by the hand to gain his confidence, to make him drunk, and to deceive him. We told them to let us alone, and keep away from us; but they followed on, and beset our paths, and they coiled themselves among us, like the snake. They poisoned us by their touch. We were not safe; we lived in danger. We were becoming like them, hypocrites and liars; all talkers and no workers.

We looked up to the Great Spirit. We went to our Father. We were encouraged. His great council gave us fair words and big promises; but we obtained no satisfaction. Things were growing worse. There were no deer in the forest. The opossum and the beaver were fled. The springs were drying up, and our people were without food to keep them from starving. We called a great council and built a big fire. The spirit of our fathers arose and spoke to us to avenge our wrongs or die. We set up the war whoop and dug up the tomahawk; our knives were ready, and the heart of Black Hawk swelled high in his bosom when he led his warriors to battle. He is satisfied. He will go to the world of spirits contented. He has done his duty. His father will meet him there and commend him. Black Hawk is a true Indian. He feels for his wife, his children, his friends, but he does not care for himself. He cares for the nation and for the Indians. They will suffer. He laments their fate.

The white men do not scalp the head, they do worse—they poison the heart. It is not pure with them. His countrymen will not be scalped, but will in a few years be like the white men, so you cannot trust them; and there must be in the white settlements as many officers as men, to take care of them and keep them in order.

Farewell, my nation! Black Hawk tried to save you, and avenge your wrongs. He drank the blood of some of the whites. He has been taken prisoner, and his plans are stopped. He can do no more! He is near his end. His sun is setting, and he will rise no more. Farewell to Black Hawk!

Keokuk, Sac and Fox, born about 1840; died December 5, 1894.

Keokuk

KEOKUK, a contemporary of Black Hawk, was one of the leaders among the Indians of the early nineteenth century. He was a member of the Sauk, which has come to be known as Sac, a tribe whose home was the upper Michigan peninsula. Their neighbors, the Fox, lived on the south shore of Lake Superior. The confederation of the Sauk and Fox resulted from attacks by the French, and dates from the early eighteenth century.

Keokuk was born on the Rock River, near Rock Island, Illinois, about 1790. He was not an hereditary chief, but rose to that position through ability. His mother was half French. Keokuk became a member of the tribal council at an early age, and was soon designated tribal guest-keeper, in which position he dispensed hospitality to tribal visitors. He used the office to further his own ambitions, became a leading councilor, and was very popular.

His passive attitude during the Black Hawk war caused him to lose prestige. However, following the defeat of Black Hawk, Keokuk was designated head chief of the Sauk when Black Hawk was deposed in 1833.

Keokuk made trips to Washington in the interest of tribal business. He was an accomplished politician and an able orator. He was too ambitious, and was easily influenced by gifts from scheming whites. In spite of this, he ably defended the rights of his people, and no doubt did as good a job as any other leader could have done.

The combined Sac and Fox tribes were moved to a reservation in Kansas in 1845, and Keokuk died at the Sauk Agency in Franklin County in the spring of 1848.

Not all the tribe-to-tribe relations were cordial and congenial, as is indicated by the following talk from a council called by the Indian agent.

The speech was made at a council held October 5, 1837, at which talks were made by the Indian peace commissioner and by representatives of the tribes present. The Sac and Fox tribes of the Mississippi and the Missouri areas and the Sioux of the Mississippi area attended the council. The *Niles Register* carried a lengthy report of the meeting and speeches of several of the Indians were printed.

The Sioux Indian chief who preceded Keokuk placed a bundle of four sticks upon the council table to signify the four occasions upon which the Sacs had violated the Sioux territory. Keokuk does not accept the charge, and proceeds to mention occasions on which the Sioux have violated the territory of the Sac and Fox Indians. He says the occasions were so numerous he would have to cut sticks for several days to secure enough tokens of violation.

"Let the Sioux Keep From Our Lands, and There Will Be Peace"

My Father: I have heard the few remarks you have made to your children. You have heard the words of those sitting around you, and you now know the way in which the hearts of the Sioux are placed.

You will now hear how my heart and the hearts of my chiefs and braves, standing around me, are placed.

I should like to know who can make these people, who have brought that bunch of sticks, speak so as to be believed.

If I were to count up everything that has taken place, on their part, it would take several days to cut sticks.

You see me, probably, for the first time. I once thought I could, myself alone, make a treaty of peace with these people.

Since the first time that I have met my white brethren in council, I have been told that the red skins must shake hands. This has always been the word.

After I returned home from the treaty of Prairie du Chien,

96

I visited these people in their lodges, and smoked their pipe; within two days they killed one of my principal braves.

They say they have a good heart. I have a good heart. I gave them a blue flag—one they professed to estimate highly. The same fall they killed one of my chief men.

My heart is good; these people do not tell the truth when they say their hearts are good.

The summer before last you wished to send one of your officers into the Sioux country. I sent two of my young chiefs, who are here, with him and your troops, as we thought it was to make peace. They brought back this pipe (holding up one); do you know it? We received it as a pipe of peace from the Sioux. Yet the same fall they killed my people on our land.

I do not think they are good men; for while my chiefs went with your troops, they killed my people on our own hunting grounds.

These people say we are deaf to your advice, and advise you to bore our ears with sticks. I think their ears are so closed against the hearing of all good, that it will be necessary to bore them with iron.

They say they are good, when they will not listen to you; nor can you make them.

I have told you that it would be useless to count up all their aggressions; that it would take several days to cut sticks. They boast of having kept quiet because you told them not to strike. Since the treaty was made they have come upon our lands and killed our men. We did not revenge ourselves, because we had given a pledge not to go on to their land.

Our difficulty with these people commenced with the drawing of the line (referring to the treaty of 1825). Before that, we kept the Sioux beyond St. Peters River. We freely hunted on the great prairie and saw nothing of them. Now they cross the line, and kill us in our own country.

97

If, among the whites, a man purchased a piece of land, another came upon it, you would drive him off. Let the Sioux keep from our lands, and there will be peace.

I now address that old man (pointing to a Sioux who had spoken). I think he does not know what his young men are now doing at home as well as he thinks he does. I will not say any thing I do not know to be true. I make no promises. If he knows his young men are, at this moment, quiet at home, he knows more than I do about mine, and must have greater powers of knowledge than I have.

I have no more to say at present. The Great Spirit has heard me, and he knows I have spoken truth. If it be not true, it is the first time that I ever told a falsehood.

Sequoyah, Cherokee, born about 1760; died August, 1843. From a sculpture, Sequoyah in typical attire, with the Cherokee syllabary which he designed.

Sequoyah

SEQUOYAH, whose gift of the Cherokee syllabary removed the shackles of illiteracy from an Indian Nation, left a mark upon all Indian history by providing a means to record and transmit the language of his people. Although unable to speak any language but Cherokee, and incapable of reading or writing anything, Sequoyah was aware of the benefits of a written word by which events could be recorded as they happened, and a precise statement made which could later be reviewed.

Work on his "talking leaves," as the symbols were called, began about 1809 and consumed most of Sequoyah's time until the system was perfected in 1821. The syllabary was proven and adopted by the Cherokees in the winter of 1821–22. Within a relatively short time all members of the Cherokee Nation could read, a printing press had been set up, and a newspaper had begun publication. Files of *The Cherokee Phoenix* from 1828 show a wide range of subjects discussed, the paper being printed partly in English and partly with the Cherokee characters, which had been cast into type.

Sequoyah's arrival upon the scene was somewhat shadowed, his birth date being placed at from 1760 to 1775. The birth dates of some of his kin have been recorded, but none was definitely set for him. He was born to Nathaniel Gist (also recorded Guest or Guess) and a Cherokee woman, in Tuskegee, Tennessee, on the Tennessee River in the Overhills country. Grant Foreman, who wrote one of the best books on Sequoyah, titled *Sequoyah*, sets his birth date at 1760.

Sequoyah, a silversmith and blacksmith, was lame as the result of a hunting accident. His work in perfecting the syllabary made a virtual recluse of him, and earned him jibes from his tribesmen. All this was changed upon the introduction of his "talking leaves," and he became a recognized leader of his people. His greatest concern was for the Cherokees. He made several trips to Washington in the interest of the Cherokee Nation, and was active in tribal governmental affairs.

Late in life Sequoyah became interested in a group of the Cherokee people who were living in Mexico and, in 1842, undertook a trip from his home in the Cherokee Nation to Mexico, in order to urge them to return to the East. It is thought he was about eighty years old at the time, and he died in Mexico in August, 1843. Members of the Cherokee tribe went to Mexico to verify the fact and report that Sequoyah was buried in the vicinity of San Fernando, Mexico.

Sequoyah was reported to have kept a diary, but it disappeared at his death. He was a shy man, and is supposed to have spoken only one time in a council meeting. He spoke on a mission to Washington, but his words came in such a torrent that the interpreter could not keep up, and sat entranced until the speech was completed. Efforts to have Sequoyah repeat the speech so it could be recorded were not successful.

The beautifully worded treaty between the Western and Eastern Cherokees which is given here was undoubtedly read in Cherokee by Sequoyah to the assembled delegates, and his mark was attached to the treaty when it was signed on August 23, 1839.

A Gift of "Talking Leaves"

Whereas our Fathers have existed as a separate and distinct Nation, in the possession and exercise of the essential and appropriate attributes of sovereignty, from a period extending into antiquity, beyond the records and memory of man, and

Whereas these attributes, with the rights and franchises which they involve, remain still in full force and virtue, as do all the national and social relations of the Cherokee people to each other and to the body politic, excepting in those particulars which have grown out of the provisions of the treaties of 1817 and 1819 between the United States and the Cherokee Nation, under which a portion of our people removed to this country and became a separate community. But the force of circumstances having recently compelled the body of the Eastern Cherokees to remove to this country, this bringing together again the two branches of the ancient Cherokee family, it has become essential to the general welfare that a union should be formed, and a system of government matured, adapted to their present condition and providing equally for the protection of each individual in the enjoyment of his rights:

Therefore we, the people composing the Eastern and Western Cherokee Nation, in National Convention assembled, by virtue of our original and inalienable rights, do hereby solemnly and mutually agree to form ourselves into one body politic, under the style and title of the Cherokee Nation.

In view of the union now formed, and for the purpose of making satisfactory adjustment of all unsettled business which may have arisen before the consummation of this union, we agree that such business shall be settled according to the provisions of the respective laws under which it originated, and the courts of the Cherokee Nation shall be governed in their decisions accordingly. Also that the delegation authorized by the Eastern Cherokees to make arrangement with Major General Scott for their removal to this country shall continue in charge of that business, with their present powers, until it shall be finally closed and also that all rights and title to public Cherokee lands on the east or west of the river Mississippi, with all other public interests which may have been vested in either branch of the Cherokee family, whether inherited from our fathers or derived from any other source, shall henceforward vest entire and unimpaired in the Cherokee Nation, as constituted by this union.

Given under our hands, at Illinois Campground, this 12th day of July, 1839.

By order of the National Convention.

GEORGE LOWREY, President of the Eastern Cherokees
GEORGE GUESS, His X Mark, President of the Western
Cherokees

(As noted, Lowrey signed the treaty, Sequoyah used his name, George Guess, and applied his mark to the agreement.)

In the search for quotations made by Sequoyah very little material has been unearthed, and this only of a few sentences. However, he was the subject of several interviews, and lengthy discussions were published as a result. In April, 1828, the *Missionary Herald* carried a report by their corresponding secretary, Jeremiah Evarts, who was a very capable writer. Evarts was one of the founders of the American Board of Commissioners for Foreign Missions and was manager for the American Bible Society. In his article Evarts reported on the progress of the Cherokee newspaper, and gave his impressions of Sequoyah, which revealed him to be an engaging person with a keen insight into the needs of the Cherokees.

The *Niles Register* of September 5, 1829, gives a lengthy resumé of a speech made by Samuel Lorenzo Knapp, a noted lecturer on literary subjects, in which he discusses in detail an interview with Sequoyah. He gives a complete account of Sequoyah's explanation of how he conceived and developed the syllabary, but not once does he give a direct quotation, since the interview was carried on through the services of an interpreter.

Albert Gallatin, who was secretary of the treasury of the United States from 1801–14, was reported to have included an interview with Sequoyah in some of his prolific writing.

John Howard Payne became interested in the Cherokees and in 1835 had Sequoyah dictate to him, again through an interpreter.

In spite of developing a method to make records of time and events, the modesty of Sequoyah has left very little upon which to base writings concerning him. The older people carried their knowledge to the grave and very little was left recorded by either the "talking leaves" or the English language to adequately trace the course of this great and humble man across the face of Cherokee and American history.

104

John Ross, Cherokee, born October 3, 1790; died August 1, 1866.
From a photograph made in Washington, D.C., in 1858.

John Ross

JOHN ROSS, bright star of the Cherokees, has been the subject of many writers, and justly so. He was one of the most tireless of the Indian workers at the time just preceding and following the tragic March of Tears, in which the tribes of the eastern part of the nation were moved to lands in what later became Oklahoma. The Indians of the South were being relentlessly pushed and crowded, and the United States government was being pressured by the whites to move the tribes west of the Mississippi.

Ross was born October 3, 1790, and was made principal chief of the Cherokees after the removal to Oklahoma. He served the Cherokees for some forty years, representing the tribes in Washington, D.C., as well as at the Cherokee capital in Tahlequah, Oklahoma. He was a man of great ability and was an outstanding citizen. He died in Washington, D.C., on August 1, 1866.

The tribes usually referred to as the Five Civilized Tribes enjoyed a high state of civilization and a benevolent form of government. They were prosperous landowners and businessmen, many with fine educations and exceptional abilities. Removal from their ancestral holdings was ruinous, and after arrival in Oklahoma, for a long period of time they were beset by many difficult problems. Relations with the different tribes were among the most vexing problems.

Ross made a plea, and continually sought for a plan to get all the tribes to work together in harmony, but in spite of his efforts, little was accomplished. In June, 1843, a council was called at Tahlequah, and it remained in session four weeks. Seventeen tribes were represented, with some ten thousand Indians present. The following speech by Ross was given at the beginning of the session, and followed by a resolution receiving little support.

"By Peace Our Condition Has Been Improved in the Pursuit of Civilized Life"

Brothers: The talk of our forefathers has been spoken, and you have listened to it. You have also smoked the pipe of peace, and shaken the right hand of friendship around the Great Councilfire, newly kindled at Tahlequah, in the west, and our hearts have been made glad on the interesting occasion.

Brothers: When we look into the history of our race, we see some green spots that are pleasing to us. We also find many things to make the heart sad. When we look upon the first council-fire kindled by our forefathers, when the pipe of peace was smoked in brotherly friendship between the different nations of red people, our hearts rejoice in the goodness of our Creator in having thus united the heart and hand of the red man in peace.

For it is in peace only that our women and children can enjoy happiness and increase in numbers.

By peace our condition has been improved in the pursuit of civilized life. We should, therefore, extend the hand of friendship from tribe to tribe, until peace shall be established between every nation of red men within the reach of our voice.

Brothers: When we call to mind the only associations which endeared us to the land which gave birth to our ancestors, where we have been brought up in peace to taste the benefits of civilized life; and when we see that our ancient fire has there been extinguished, and our people compelled to remove to a new and distant country, we cannot but feel sorry; but the designs of Providence, in the course of events, are mysterious—we should not, therefore, despair of once more enjoying the blessings of peace in our new homes.

Brothers: By this removal, tribes that were once separated by distance have become neighbors, and some of them, hitherto not known to each other, have met and become acquainted. There are, however, numerous other tribes to whom we are still strangers.

Brothers: It is for reviving here in the west the ancient talk of our forefathers, and of perpetuating for ever the old fire and pipe of peace brought from the east, and of extending them from nation to nation, and for adopting such international laws as may be necessary to redress the wrongs which may be done by individuals of our respective nations upon each other, that you have been invited to attend the present council.

Brothers: Let us so then act that the peace and friendship which so happily existed between our forefathers, may be for ever preserved; and that we may always live as brothers of the same family.

At the time of the War Between the States, feeling of the citizens, both Indian and white, was divided in allegiance to the Union and to the Confederate States. The Territory, later to become part of Oklahoma, had partisans for both of the contestants. Some of the Indians became active in support of the South, others sided with the North.

The Cherokees chose to side with the South, and this is John Ross's address to the Cherokee National Assembly, setting out the course of action to be taken by the Cherokees. This speech was delivered at Tahlequah on October 9, 1861, and was taken from a rare pamphlet printed at Tahlequah by the Cherokee Nation. The copy used as reference is in the Frank Phillips Collection at the University of Oklahoma Library.

"The Cherokee People Stand Upon New Ground"

Friends and Fellow Citizens:

Since the last meeting of the National Council, events have occurred that will occupy a prominent place in the history of the world. The United States have been dissolved and two governments now exist. Twelve of the States composing the late Union have erected themselves into a government under the style of the Confederate States of America, and as you know, are now engaged in a war for their independence. The contest thus far has been attended with success, almost uninterrupted on their side, and marked by brilliant victories. Of its final result there seems to be no ground for a reasonable doubt. The unanimity and devotion of the people of the Confederate States must sooner or later secure their success over all opposition and result in the establishment of their independence and a recognition of it by the other nations of the Earth.

At the beginning of the conflict, I felt that the interests of the Cherokee people would be best maintained by remaining quiet and not involving themselves in it prematurely. Our relations had long existed with the United States Government and bound us to observe amity and peace alike with all the States. Neutrality was proper and wise so long as there remained a reasonable probability that the difficulty between the two sections of the Union would be settled, as a different course would have placed all our rights in jeopardy and might have led to the sacrifice of the people.

But when there was no longer any reason to believe that the Union of the States would be continued, there was no cause to hesitate as to the course the Cherokee Nation should pursue. Our geographical position and domestic institutions allied us to the South, while the developments daily made in our vicinity and as to the purposes of the war waged against the Confederate States clearly pointed out the path of interest. These considerations produced a unanimity of sentiment among the people as to the policy to be adopted by the Cherokee Nation, which was clearly expressed in their general meeting held at Tahlequah on the 21st day of August last. A copy of the proceedings of that meeting is submitted for your information.

In accordance with the declarations embodied in the Resolutions then adopted, the Executive Council deemed it proper to exercise the authority conferred upon them by the people there assembled. Messengers were dispatched to General Albert Pike, the distinguished Indian Commissioner of the Confederate States, who, having negotiated treaties with the neighboring Indian Nations, was then establishing relations between his government and the Comanches and other Indians in the Southwest, who bore a copy of the proceedings of the meeting referred to, and a letter from the Executive Authorities, proposing on behalf of the Nation to enter into a Treaty of Alliance, defensive and offensive, with the Confederate States. In the exercise of the same general Authority and to be ready as far as practicable to meet any emergency that might spring upon our northern border, it was thought proper to raise a regiment of mounted men and tender its service to General McCulloch.

The people responded with alacrity to the call, and it is believed the regiment will be found as efficient as any other like number of men. It is now in the service of the Confederate States for the purpose of aiding in defending their homes and the common rights of the Indian Nations about us. This regiment is composed of ten full companies, and in addition to the force previously authorized to be raised to operate outside of the Nation by General McCulloch, will show that the Cherokee people are ready to do all in their power in defense of the Confederate cause which has now become their own. And it is to be hoped that our people will spare no means to sustain them, but contribute liberally to supply any want of comfortable clothing for the approaching season.

In years long since past, our ancestors met undaunted those who would invade their mountain homes beyond the Mississippi; let not their descendants of the present day be found unworthy

111

of them, or unable to stand by the chivalrous men of the South by whose side they may be called to fight in self defense.

The Cherokee people do not desire to be involved in war, but self preservation fully justifies them in the course they have adopted, and they will be recreant to themselves if they do not sustain it to the utmost of their humble abilities.

A Treaty with the Confederate States has been entered into and is now submitted for your ratification. In view of the circumstances by which we are surrounded, and the provisions of the Treaty, it will be found to be the most important ever negotiated on behalf of the Cherokee Nation, and will mark a new era in its history. Without attempting a recapitulation of all its provisions, some of its distinguishing features may be briefly enumerated.

The relations of the Cherokee Nation are changed from the United to the Confederate States, with guarantees of protection, and a recognition in future negotiations only of its Constitutional Authorities. The metes and boundaries as defined by Patent from the United States are continued and a guaranty given for the Neutral Land, or a fair consideration in case it should be lost by war or negotiation, and an advance thereon to pay the National debt, and to meet other contingencies. The payment of all our annuities and the security of our investments are provided for. The jurisdiction of the Cherokee Courts over all members of the Nation, whether by birth, marriage, or adoption is recognized.

Our title to our lands is placed beyond dispute. Our relations with the Confederate States is that of a Ward; theirs to us that of a Protectorate with powers restricted. The District Court, with a limited civil and criminal jurisdiction, is admitted into the Country instead of being located in Van Buren as was the United States Court. This is, perhaps, one of the most important provisions of the Treaty and secures to our own citizens the great Constitutional right of trial by a jury of their own vicinage, and releases them from the petty abuses and vexations of the old system before a foreign jury and in a foreign country. It gives us a Delegate in Congress on the same footing with Delegates from the Territories by which our interests can be represented—a right which has long been withheld from the Nation and which has imposed upon it a large expense and great injustice. It also contains reasonable stipulation in regard to the appointment powers of the Agent, and in regard to licensed traders. The Cherokee Nation may be called upon to furnish troops for the defense of the Indian country, but is never to be taxed for the support of any war in which the States may be engaged.

The Cherokee people stand upon new ground. Let us hope that the clouds which overspread the land will be dispersed, and that we shall prosper as we have never before done. New avenues to usefulness and distinction will be opened to the ingenuous youth of the Country. Our rights of self government will be more fully recognized, and our citizens be no longer dragged off upon flimsy pretexts to be imprisoned and tried before distant tribunals. No just cause exists for domestic difficulties. Let them be buried with the past and only mutual friendship and harmony be cherished.

Our relations with the neighboring tribes are of the most friendly character. Let us see that the white path which leads from our country to theirs be obstructed by no act of ours, and that it be open to all those with whom we may be brought into intercourse.

Amid the excitement of the times, it is to be hoped that the interests of education will not be allowed to suffer and that no interruption be brought into the usual operations of the Government. Let all its officers continue to discharge their appropriate duties. As the services of some of your members may be required elsewhere and all unnecessary expense should be avoided, I respectfully recommend that the business of the session be promptly discharged.

Seattle, Suquamish, born 1786; died June 7, 1866.

Seattle

SEATTLE, chief of the Suquamish and Duwamish tribes, has been given honors that few other Indians have received. The thriving metropolis of Seattle, Washington, was named for him; there is a bronze statue in Seattle commemorating this fact, and each year the Boy Scouts have a memorial ceremony at his tomb at Suquamish, Washington.

Seattle, and his father before him, were friends of the whites and eager to help them in any manner. Catholic missionaries converted Seattle in the 1830s, and he demonstrated his belief by the way he lived. He was the first signer of the Port Elliott Treaty in 1855, by which the Washington tribes were given a reservation. The Suquamish were allied with several smaller tribes in what is now Washington and Oregon. Seattle was born in 1786, and died June 7, 1866.

The speech given here was taken down by Dr. Henry Smith, a man of some talent, who mastered the Duwamish language in about two years. Dr. Smith has done us a great service in preserving this address, which may cause some present day citizens to wonder at Seattle's predictions.

The Washington Territory was organized in 1853. A plat for the town of Seattle was filed, and the first post office was put into use. Governor Stevens soon visited Seattle, and upon the occasion made an address to the settlers and Indians gathered in the small community. After his talk, Seattle made his reply, which was delivered through an interpreter. Dr. Smith carefully wrote it down on the spot.

Yonder sky that has wept tears of compassion upon my people for centuries untold, and which to us appears changeless and eternal, may change. Today is fair. Tomorrow it may be overcast with clouds. My words are like the stars that never change. Whatever Seattle says the great chief at Washington can rely upon with as much certainty as he can upon the return of the sun or the seasons. The White Chief says that Big Chief at Washington sends us greetings of friendship and goodwill. This is kind of him for we know he has little need of our friendship in return. His people are many. They are like the grass that covers vast prairies. My people are few. They resemble the scattering trees of a storm-swept plain. The great—and I presume—good White Chief sends us word that he wishes to buy our lands but is willing to allow us enough to live comfortably. This indeed appears just, even generous, for the Red Man no longer has rights that he need respect, and the offer may be wise also, as we are no longer in need of an extensive country.

There was a time when our people covered the land as the waves of a wind-ruffled sea cover its shell paved floor, but that time long since passed away with the greatness of tribes that are now but a mournful memory. I will not dwell on, nor mourn over, our untimely decay, nor reproach my paleface brothers with hastening it as we too may have been somewhat to blame.

Youth is impulsive. When our young men grow angry at some real or imaginary wrong, and disfigure their faces with black paint, it denotes that their hearts are black, and that they are often cruel and relentless, and our old men and old women are unable to restrain them. Thus it has ever been. Thus it was when the white man first began to push our forefathers westward. But let us hope that the hostilities between us may never return. We would have everything to lose and nothing to gain. Revenge by young men is considered gain, even at the cost of their own lives, but old men who stay at home in times of war, and mothers who have sons to lose, know better.

Our good father at Washington—for I presume he is now our father as well as yours, since King George has moved his boundaries further north—our great and good father, I say, sends us word that if we do as he desires he will protect us. His brave warriors will be to us a bristling wall of strength, and his wonderful ships of war will fill our harbors so that our ancient enemies far to the northward—the Hydas and Tsimpsians—will cease to frighten our women, children and old men. Then in reality will he be our father and we his children. But can that ever be? Your God is not our God! Your God loves your people and hates mine. He folds his strong protecting arms lovingly about the pale face and leads him by the hand as a father leads his infant son—but He has forsaken His red children—if they really are His. Our God, the Great Spirit, seems also to have forsaken us. Your God makes your people wax strong every day. Soon they will fill all the land. Our people are ebbing away like a rapidly receding tide that will never return. The white man's God cannot love our people or He would protect them. They seem to be orphans who can look nowhere for help. How then can we be brothers? How can your God become our God and renew our prosperity and awaken in us dreams of returning greatness. If we have a common heavenly father He must be partial—for He came to His paleface children. We never saw Him. He gave you laws but had no word for his red children whose teeming multitudes once filled this vast continent as stars fill the firmament. No; we are two distinct races with separate origins and separate destinies. There is little in common between us.

To us the ashes of our ancestors are sacred and their resting place is hallowed ground. You wander far from the graves of your ancestors and seemingly without regret. Your religion was written upon tables of stone by the iron finger of your God so that you could not forget. The Red Man could never comprehend nor remember it. Our religion is the traditions of our ancestors—the dreams of our old men, given them in the solemn hours of night by the Great Spirit; and the visions of our sachems, and is written in the hearts of our people.

Your dead cease to love you and the land of their nativity as soon as they pass the portals of the tomb and wander way beyond the stars. They are soon forgotten and never return. Our dead never forget the beautiful world that gave them being. They still love its verdant valleys, its murmuring rivers, its magnificent mountains, sequestered vales and verdant lined lakes and bays, and ever yearn in tender, fond affection over the lonely hearted living, and often return from the Happy Hunting Ground to visit, guide, console and comfort them.

Day and night cannot dwell together. The Red Man has ever fled the approach of the White Man, as the morning mist flees before the morning sun.

However, your proposition seems fair and I think that my people will accept it and will retire to the reservation you offer them. Then we will dwell in peace, for the words of the Great White Chief seem to be the words of nature speaking to my people out of dense darkness.

It matters little where we pass the remnant of our days. They will not be many. The Indians' night promises to be dark. Not a single star of hope hovers above his horizon. Sad-voiced winds moan in the distance. Grim fate seems to be on the Red Man's trail, and wherever he goes he will hear the approaching footsteps of his fell destroyer and prepare stolidly to meet his doom, as does the wounded doe that hears the approaching footsteps of the hunter.

A few more moons. A few more winters—and not one of the descendants of the mighty hosts that once moved over this broad land or lived in happy homes, protected by the Great Spirit, will remain to mourn over the graves of a people—once more powerful and hopeful than yours. But why should I mourn at the untimely fate of my people? Tribe follows tribe, and nation follows nation, like the waves of the sea. It is the order of nature, and regret is useless. Your time of decay may be distant, but it will surely come, for even the White Man whose God walked and talked with him as friend with friend, cannot be exempt from the common destiny. We may be brothers after all. We will see.

We will ponder your proposition and when we decide we will let you know. But should we accept it, I here and now make this condition that we will not be denied the privilege without molestation of visiting at any time the tombs of our ancestors, friends and children. Every part of this soil is sacred in the estimation of my people. Every hillside, every valley, every plain and grove, has been hallowed by some sad or happy event in days long vanished. Even the rocks, which seem to be dumb and dead as they swelter in the sun along the silent shore, thrill with memories of stirring events connected with the lives of my people, and the very dust upon which you now stand responds more lovingly to their footsteps than to yours, because it is rich with the blood of our ancestors and our bare feet are conscious of the sympathetic touch. Our departed braves, fond mothers, glad, happy-hearted maidens, and even our little children who lived here and rejoiced here for a brief season, will love these somber solitudes and at eventide they greet shadowy returning spirits. And when the last Red Man shall have perished, and the memory of my tribe shall have become a myth among the White Men, these shores will swarm with the invisible dead of my tribe, and when your children's children think themselves alone in the field, the store, the shop, upon the highway, or in the silence of the pathless woods, they will not be alone. In all the earth there is no place dedicated to solitude. At night when the streets of your cities and villages are silent and you think them deserted, they will throng with the returning hosts that once filled them and still love this beautiful land. The White Man will never be alone.

Let him be just and deal kindly with my people, for the dead are not powerless. Dead, did I say? There is no death, only a change of worlds.

Washakie, Shoshone, born 1798; died February 20, 1900.

Washakie

WASHAKIE and his Shoshones have a long history of friendship with the whites. Washakie, who was born in 1798, served the United States armed forces with such distinction that a frontier army post was named in his honor. Camp Augur, which was established in the Wind River Valley on June 28, 1869, after a series of name changes became Fort Washakie in December of 1878. The fort was abandoned in 1899, and control of the property was relinquished in 1909.

In the treaty at Fort Bridger in 1868, Washakie and his Shoshones and the Bannocks were given their reservation. The Arapahoes started living on the reserve in 1877. The original treaty by which the reservation was set up is in the courthouse in Evanston, Wyoming.

Washakie was killed in personal combat with a Crow chief on February 20, 1900. He was buried with the military honors due a captain in the post cemetery at Fort Washakie. A stone on his grave indicates the dates of 1804–1900, but other data support his birth date as being 1798.

Observers of his era said that Washakie understood the history of his times better than many statesmen. President Ulysses S. Grant gave him a silver-mounted saddle in appreciation of his services to the army.

The speech here was made by Washakie to the members of his tribe during a visit by Mormon missionaries. The elders of the tribe were reluctant to heed the words of the missionaries attempting to teach them religion. They insisted that instead of the Book of Mormon the missionaries should bring them food, tools, and ammunition, which they could use at once.

Washakie chides his tribal advisers as the Shoshones and Mormons met in the summer of 1855 on Horse Creek, in Idaho.

125

You are all fools, you are blind, and cannot see; you have no ears, for you do not hear; you are fools for you do not understand. These men are our friends. The great Mormon captain has talked with our Father above the clouds, and He told the Mormon captain to send these men here to tell us the truth, and not a lie.

They have not got forked tongues. They talk straight, with one tongue, and tell us that after a few more snows the buffalo will be gone, and if we do not learn some other way to get something to eat, we will starve to death.

Now, we know that is the truth, for this country was once covered with buffalo, elk, deer and antelope, and we had plenty to eat, and also robes for bedding, and to make lodges. But now, since the white man has made a road across our land, and has killed off our game, we are hungry, and there is nothing for us to eat. Our women and children cry for food and we have no food to give them.

The time was when our Father, who lives above the clouds, loved our fathers, who lived long ago, and His face was bright, and He talked with our fathers. His face shone upon them, and their skins were white like the white man's. Then they were wise and wrote books, and the Great Father talked good to them; but after a while our people would not hear Him, and they quarreled and stole and fought, until the Great Father got mad, because His children would not hear Him talk.

Then He turned His face away from them, and His back to them, and that caused a shade to come over them, and that is why our skin is black and our minds dark. That darkness came because the Great Father's back was toward us, and now we cannot see as the white man sees. We can make a bow and arrow, but the white man's mind is strong and light.

The white man can make this (picking up a Colt's revolver), and a little thing that he carries in his pocket, so that he can tell where the sun is on a dark day, and when it is night he can tell when it will come daylight. This is because the face of the Father is towards him, and His back is towards us. But after a while the Great Father will quit being mad, and will turn his face towards us. Then our skin will be light.

Chief Joseph, Nez Perce, born about 1840; died September 21, 1904.

Chief Joseph

CHIEF JOSEPH of the Nez Percés wrote a record of leadership that has attracted many writers and historians. Not a large tribe, the Nez Percés lived in the northwest mountainous country, and were generally at peace with their neighboring tribes and with the whites. As infiltration of settlers increased and the pressure upon the Indians became heavier, they resented the intrusion as did the other Indians.

Joseph, born in 1840, was an hereditary chieftain, and assumed his position as chief and village leader at about thirty-one years of age. He was six feet tall, strong and active, and possessed strength of character and a pleasing personality which made him a strong leader and won him the friendship of many important white people.

Joseph made his most impressive mark on history as the leader of the Nez Percés in their attempt to escape from the United States into Canada in 1877. In eleven weeks of flight his tribe covered some sixteen hundred miles through the rugged country of the Northwest, engaged ten separate United States military commands in thirteen battles and skirmishes, and in almost every case defeated them or fought them to a standstill. Superb maneuvering found the Indians a bare thirty miles from the Canadian border when conditions became so severe that Chief Joseph submitted to surrender to General Oliver O. Howard and General Nelson A. Miles.

Describing the campaign, General William T. Sherman said it was "one of the most extraordinary wars of which there is any record."

Joseph visited in Washington and the East in 1903. The following year, on September 21, 1904, the matchless tactician started on the longest journey of all, when he departed this life for good.

The speech here was made on the occasion of the Nez Percé surrender to Generals Howard and Miles, October 5, 1877.

129

"I Will Fight No More Forever"

Tell General Howard I know his heart. What he told me before, I have in my heart. I am tired of fighting. Our chiefs are killed. Looking Glass is dead. Toohoolhoolzote* is dead. The old men are all dead. It is the young men who say yes and no. He who led on the young men is dead. It is cold and we have no blankets. The little children are freezing to death. My people, some of them, have run away to the hills and have no blankets, no food; no one knows where they are—perhaps freezing to death. I want to have time to look for my children and see how many I can find. Maybe I shall find them among the dead. Hear me, my chiefs. I am tired; my heart is sick and sad. From where the sun now stands I will fight no more forever.

*Elsewhere Too-hool-hool-suit.

Black Kettle, Cheyenne, birth date unknown; died November 27, 1868.

Black Kettle

BLACK KETTLE was a principal chief of the Cheyennes, and his group of Indians ranged in the area between the Platte and Arkansas rivers, including Colorado, Nebraska, Kansas, and Oklahoma. They at one time lived on a reservation in Colorado adjoining an allotment for the Arapahoes. The Cheyennes were a warlike people, ranging far and wide over their hunting ground. George Bird Grinnell has written a fine book appropriately titled *The Fighting Cheyennes*, which follows the movements and actions of these people.

The speech given below was made October 12, 1865, at a council on the Little Arkansas River, when the United States government was negotiating a treaty with the Cheyennes and Arapahoes. General J. B. Sanborn was the president of the peace commission and conducted the council. The Mrs. Wilmarth to whom Black Kettle refers was the interpreter for the Cheyennes.[1]

On November 29, 1864, the Cheyenne village on Sand Creek near the reservation was attacked by the forces of Major John M. Chivington and the action became known as the Sand Creek Massacre. Although he was reported killed, Black Kettle was one of the survivors and his speech at the Little Arkansas indicated compliance with the white man's wishes. Nevertheless, things did not go smoothly for the Cheyennes, and they continued depredations over much of their territory.

[1] Mrs. Margaret Wilmarth was the former wife of the late Major Thomas Fitzpatrick, who died while serving as agent for the Arapahoes. Fitzpatrick was a noted Western explorer, guide, hunter, trapper, and friend of the Indians. He was often referred to as "Broken Hand" Fitzpatrick following the explosion of a rifle barrel which caused him to lose three fingers of his right hand. While he participated in many skirmishes against various tribes of Indians, the speeches by Indians at this council in 1865 attest to the high regard the Arapahoes had for Major Fitzpatrick, and they transferred their respect to his widow.

Black Kettle moved with many of his people to a location on the Washita River in Indian Territory (Oklahoma). There, on the morning of November 27, 1868, in an attack led by General George A. Custer, the village was obliterated, and Black Kettle was among the large number of Indians killed.

Here is Black Kettle's reply to the Indian commissioners at the Little Arkansas council:

"We Want the Privilege of Crossing the Arkansas to Kill Buffalo"

The Great Father above hears us, and the Great Father at Washington will hear what we say. Is it true that you came here from Washington, and is it true what you say here today? The Big Chief he give his words to me to come and meet you here, and I take hold and retain what he says. I believe all to be true, and think it is all true. Their young white men, when I meet them on the plains, I give them my horse and my moccasins, and I am glad today to think that the Great Father has sent good men to take pity on us.

Your young soldiers I don't think they listen to you. You bring presents, and when I come to get them I am afraid they will strike me before I get away. When I come in to receive presents I take them up crying. Although wrongs have been done me, I live in hopes. I have not got two hearts. These young men, (Cheyennes) when I call them into the lodge and talk with them, they listen to me and mind what I say. Now we are again together to make peace. My shame (mortification) is as big as the earth, although I will do what my friends advise me to do. I once thought that I was the only man that persevered to be the friend of the white man, but since they have come and cleaned out (robbed) our lodges, horses, and everything else, it is hard for me to believe white men any more.

Here we are, altogether, Arapahoes and Cheyennes, but few

134

of us, we are one people. As soon as you arrived you started runners after us and the Arapahoes, with words that I took hold of immediately on hearing them. From what I can see around me, I feel confident that our Great Father has taken pity on me, and I feel that it is the truth all that has been told me today. All my friends—the Indians that are holding back—they are afraid to come in; are afraid they will be betrayed as I have been. I am not afraid of white men, but come and take you by the hand, and am glad to have an opportunity of so doing. These lands that you propose to give us I know nothing about. There is but a handful here now of the Cheyenne nation, and I would rather defer making any permanent treaty until the others come. We are living friendly now.

There are a great many white men. Possibly you may be looking for some one with a strong heart. Possibly you may be intending to do something for me better than I know of.

Inasmuch as my Great Father has sent you here to take us by the hand, why is it that we are prevented from crossing the Arkansas? If we give you our hands in peace, we give them also to those of the plains. We want the privilege of crossing the Arkansas to kill buffalo. I have but few men here, but what I say to them they listen, and they will abide by their promise whatever it may be. All these young soldiers are taking us by the hand, and I hope it will come back good times as formerly. It is very hard to have one-half of our nation absent at this time; we wish to get through at once. My friends, I want you to understand that I have sent up north for my people, and I want the road open for them to get here. I hope that which you have said will be just as you have told me, and I am glad to hear such good counsel from you. When my friends get down from the north I think it will be the best time to talk about the lands. There are so few here it would not look right to make a treaty for the whole nation, and so many absent. I hope you will use your influence with the troops to open a road for my men to get here. You may mark out the lands you propose giving us, but I know nothing about them; it is a new country to me.

I have been in great hopes that I may see my children that were taken prisoners last fall, and when I get here I do not see them. I feel disappointed. My young men here, and friends, when we meet in council and come to the conclusion, it is the truth, we do not vary from it.

This lady's husband (Mrs. Wilmarth, formerly Fitzpatrick), Major Fitzpatrick, when he was our agent and brought us presents he did not take them into forts and houses, but would drive his wagons into our villages and empty them there. Every one would help themselves and feel glad. He has gone ahead of us, and he told us that when he was gone we would have trouble, and it has proved true. We are sorry. But since the death of Major Fitzpatrick we have had many agents. I don't know as we have been wronged, but it looks so. The amount of goods has diminished; it don't look right. Has known Colonel Leavenworth for some time; he has treated me well; whether it will continue or not I do not know. He has got a strong heart, and has done us a great deal of good. Now that times are so uncertain in this country I would like to have my old friend Colonel Bent with me.

This young man, Charles Wrath, does not get tired. He is always ready to go and meet them and give them whatever news he has to send to them. There may be wrongs done, but we want to show who does these wrongs before you censure us. I feel that the Great Father has taken pity on us, and that ever since we have met Colonel Leavenworth's words have been true, and nothing done since that time but what is true.

I heard that some chiefs were sent here to see us. We have brought our women and children, and now we want to see if you are going to have pity on us.

This is all by Black Kettle.

Little Raven, Arapaho, born about 1820; died, 1889.

Little Raven

LITTLE RAVEN was one of the most noted of the Arapaho leaders. During his life he ranged the high plains and western areas and was well known among the other tribes with whom the Arapahoes had contact. The Arapahoes were called the Blue Bead or Big Bead Indians because of the turquoise beads of which they were especially fond and which they wore as ornaments.

Little Raven married a Kiowa-Apache woman in 1840; assuming that he was about twenty years old at that time, his birth year was about 1820.

Little Raven attended the Medicine Lodge council in 1867, and an article by Alfred A. Taylor in *The Chronicles of Oklahoma*, 1924, Volume II, gives his impressions of the distinguished Indian chief. Taylor wrote: "Towering above all in native intellect and oratory— exact image of Andrew Johnson—barring his color, Little Raven, chief of the Arapahoes, was there. His speech before the commissioners on the question of damages, back annuities, and the cause of the war would have done credit to an enlightened statesman."

Little Raven was the first signer for the Arapahoes of the Fort Wise, Colorado, Treaty on February 18, 1861. He took part in the Cheyenne and Arapaho war on the Kansas border, but agreed to the Medicine Lodge Treaty.

After the Medicine Lodge council, all of Little Raven's efforts were directed toward keeping his people at peace with the government and leading them toward civilization. Even though their allies, the Kiowas and Cheyennes, went on the warpath, Little Raven's influence kept the Arapahoes at peace with the whites.

Little Raven died at Cantonment, Oklahoma, in the winter of

1889, after more than twenty years as the leader of the progressive element among the Arapahoes.

In the fall of 1865 a peace commission met at a camp on the Little Arkansas River, with instructions to negotiate a treaty with the Arapaho, Apache, Cheyenne, Comanche, and Kiowa Indians. The sessions began on October 12 and continued through October 14, with General J. B. Sanborn as president of the treaty commission. Other members of the commission included General W. S. Harney, Superintendent Thomas Murray, Colonel Kit Carson, Colonel William W. Bent, Indian Agent J. H. Leavenworth, and Judge James Steele.

One of the interpreters was Mrs. Margaret Wilmarth, who had been the wife of the late Major Fitzpatrick, who died while serving as agent to the Arapahoes. He was well liked, and the Indians transferred their affection to his widow, who had remarried.

Little Raven spoke, and in his opening remarks stated that the last time they had met, there were 390 lodges. Since that time, he said, many young men had married and there were additional lodges. He continued:

"It Is Our Great Desire and Wish to Make a Good, Permanent Peace"

This is the wife (Mrs. Margaret Wilmarth) of Major Fitzpatrick, who died in Washington city. He was our first agent. When Major Fitzpatrick came, he came and inquired for his children, the Cheyennes and Arapahoes, and sent for them, and said he wanted to make a good word for them.

The Great Spirit above gave them this ground, but afterwards some writing came from Washington; he brought it and explained it to us, what it was. When Major Fitzpatrick first came, he married this woman, (Mrs. Wilmarth) he laid off certain country on the North Platte, commencing at the junction of the North and South Platte, running thence along the North Platte to the summit of the principal range of the Rocky Mountains, then along said range in a southerly direction to the Arkansas river, thence down said river to the Cimarron crossing, then north to the place of beginning.

Major Fitzpatrick then came again, and they were called to another meeting on the Platte; then some tracts of land were talked of, and some of the Indians objected to signing the treaty of 1851.

After a long time there was another change of administration. Greenwood was sent to them. We did not understand him. I kept out of all fights and troubles. Now, this day, you have come from the President, we are glad; we take you by the hand, and we are glad to have an opportunity of so doing.

Here are our young men and friends with us; words shall not be thrown on the ground, but shall be kept by us.

Tell the President just as we say. Inasmuch as you have come from the President, in council, we wish you to hear and understand us. It is our great desire and wish to make a good, permanent peace. Inasmuch as you come from the President, you come with truth; you have come to save the remnant of our nation. You propose to give us land where we can live in quiet; we accept your proposal, and we hope, as you are our friends and friends of our brothers the Cheyennes here, that you will see that it is faithfully carried out.

I now desire a choice of lands. I think the selection of lands for the halfbreeds should be in the old reservation near Fort Lyon. Yesterday you spoke of a reservation north of the North Platte, or south of the Arkansas. North of the North Platte has once been given to the Sioux to my knowledge; south of the Arkansas has been given to the Comanches and Kiowas. To place them on the same ground would be to make prisoners of us, or like going out of one fire into another.

I understand that this commission has a quantity of goods coming. I look at this as a present for myself and my children. I am satisfied to take you by the hand, and will not be the first one to break the treaty. There are men whom I knew when I was a boy (indicating Colonels Bent and Carson).

The Sioux in the north, and the Comanches in the south, were the first to commence the war, and then we were drawn into it.

As soon as you got here you sent runners and notified us of your arrival. We felt as though there was something good, and we hastened to come immediately. Where the antelope and buffalo live is country where I want to live; that is what I raise my children on, and the way I get my support: hunting.

The lands you speak of and describe to us, we observe and accept them, but we prefer to leave them there for the present, and live on the unoccupied lands of our old homes, until you have acquired such a title to them from other Indians as will enable us to live on them in peace, and until our Great Father shall be of the opinion that it will be better for us to go to them.

There is something very strong for us—that fool band of soldiers that cleared out our lodges, and killed our women and children. This is strong (hard) on us. There, at Sand Creek, is one chief, Left Hand; White Antelope and many other chiefs lie there; our women and children lie there. Our lodges were destroyed there, and our horses were taken from us there, and I do not feel disposed to go right off in a new country and leave them. What I have to say, I am glad to see you writing down to take to the Big Chief in Washington.

Our families and our old men that I left out at our village, I will inform them of what I have done as soon as I get there. This summer, fall, and winter, I shall not see the Arkansas river; after that I shall start off at a distance, and look at the country south of the Arkansas and see it, when the troops get out of this country; then I expect to cross the Arkansas and come into this country.

I expect this commission will give us two traders this winter, and the Cheyennes to stay and live with us and trade with us.

Charles Rath is one that we want, and Colonel William W. Bent is the other that we want to go with us this winter.

When Colonel Leavenworth gets goods again I expect to be ready to meet him.

In June, 1871, a group of Cheyenne, Arapaho, and Wichita Indian chiefs were sent on a visit to Washington. They also visited New York and Boston, and made speeches to large gatherings of whites who were interested in the welfare of the Indians. The speech given here was delivered by Little Raven at the Cooper Union in New York. Little Raven was the first Indian speaker, and he stood behind a desk as he spoke, with an interpreter repeating his words in English, sentence by sentence. The audience was very attentive, and applauded generously.

"My People Are Waiting on the Hills to Greet Me When I Return"

I have come from a long distance to see my friends. Years ago, when I was at home, they told me that I had a home here, and father and mother. I have come now to find them. When at home, in my camp, a letter came from the Father at Washington, asking me to come and see him away in the States. I had been waiting for it for a long time, and when it came I did not hesitate a moment, but came at once. I felt that the Father at Washington would right the wrongs of myself and my people. In this letter they told me I had many friends in this country who never saw the Indians, and who would be glad to see them.

I talked with the chiefs of the other tribes, and we came here to see you tonight. Before leaving, I told my young people to remain with the agency till I came home, when I hoped to bring them good news. I told them I would be gone forty or fifty nights; they will expect me when that time is passed. They think I will look like a white man when I come back, because I have been to see the white man in the big house.

143

I am glad to see so many of my friends here tonight, so many gentlemen, chiefs, and ladies. I think the Great Spirit has something to do with bringing you all here tonight. Long ago the Arapahoes had a fine country of their own. The white man came to see them, and the Indians gave him buffalo meat and a horse to ride on, and they told him the country was big enough for the white man and the Arapahoes, too.

After a while the white men found gold in our country. They took the gold and pushed the Indian from his home. I thought Washington would make it all right. I am an old man now. I have been waiting many years for Washington to give us our rights. The Government sent agents and soldiers out there to us, and both have driven us from our lands. We do not want to fight. The white man has taken away everything.

I want to tell you of this, because I believe if you know it you will correct the evil. I think the Great Spirit is looking at all that is said here, and for that reason I am talking the truth. I want my people to live like white people, and have the same chance. I hope the Great Spirit will put a good heart into the white people, that they may give us our rights. When I saw the old man (Peter Cooper) who invited us to come here tonight, my heart opened to him. I have thanked the Great Spirit many times that I have been permitted to be here.

I want to tell you all that is in my heart, and if I do not it will be because I hide it. We want to travel the same road as the white man. We want to have his rifle, his powder, and his ball to hunt with. My people are waiting on the hills to greet me when I return, and I want to give them a good report.

Lone Wolf, Kiowa, birth date unrecorded; died, 1879.

Lone Wolf

LONE WOLF was one of the prominent leaders of the Kiowas, and participated in several treaty sessions. His birth was not recorded, and so far as can be learned no age was indicated at the time of his death in 1879.

Many of the noted Indians came into public notice quite suddenly, and no indication has been given of when or where they were born, where they spent their youth, or any other events until they were in the frontier limelight.

Lone Wolf was head chief of the Kiowas in 1879. As was the custom among many of the tribes, he gave his name to a younger man, his nephew, who was still recognized as a leader among the Kiowas in 1896.

In the winter of 1873–74, Lone Wolf's two sons (actually, one son and one nephew) were killed while on a raid into Mexico. Lone Wolf went to Mexico to bury the young men, and from that time was hostile to the whites.

Among the councils attended by Lone Wolf was one held at Fort Sill, Oklahoma, on October 6, 1873. The speech given here was delivered at a council held several years earlier at the Big Bend of the Arkansas River in Kansas. The Kiowas of the Upper Arkansas met with representatives of the Indian Commissioner on November 26, 1866.

Lone Wolf was among the group of famous Indian chiefs and warriors who made the disastrous attack on the hunters who were forted up at Adobe Walls in West Texas. He was fighting with the Kiowa-Apache group.

The council at which Lone Wolf spoke in 1866 was attended by Captain Charles Bogy, W. R. Irwin, and J. H. Leavenworth, special

Indian agents, and David Lewers, interpreter. The official secretary recorded proceedings and made an interesting comment on the ritual preceding Lone Wolf's talk.

The secretary of the peace council wrote in his report: "The Indians then laid two pieces of paper on the floor—one blue and one white. Otank, or White-Bird, an old Indian, then went through a form of prayer, and spoke as follows to Lone Wolf, in Kiowa, who repeated it to the interpreter in Comanche."

In the official report of the council, Lone Wolf is credited with making the speech, except for the notation made by the secretary. Lone Wolf had expressed himself as friendly and anxious to preserve peace.

Recorded for the official report, here is the speech:

"I Am the Man That Makes It Rain"

That piece of paper (pointing to the white) represents the earth. There is a big water all around the earth. The circular blue paper is the sky. The sun goes around the earth. The sun is our father. All the Red Men in this country, all the buffalo are all his (Lone Wolf pointed at the old man). Our Father, the sun, told us that the white men would kill all of them. There is no place for us to hide because the water is all around the earth.

When my time comes to die I intend to die and not wait to be killed by the white men. I want you to write to the Great Chief and tell him that I understand my Great Father, the sun; that my Great Father, the sun, sent me a message; that I went around the prairie poor and crying, and my Great Father, the sun, sent me a message which I can read.

A long time ago when I was little I began to study medicine, and when we make a treaty with the white man I see it and know whether it is good or not.

I am the man that makes it rain. I talk to the Great Father. If I have any difficulty with anyone and wish them to perish with thirst, I stop the rain, and if I wish them well, I cause it to rain so that the corn can grow.

My Great Father, the sun, told me that fire and water were alike, and that we cannot live without either of them.

Cochise, Apache, date of birth unknown; died June 8, 1874. This is
a photo copy of a painting of the Mescalero Apache chief.

Cochise

COCHISE, as the fabulous leader of the Apaches in the south-western United States, gave the U.S. Army hell for years. The Apaches knew every canyon and valley, every hill and crag, every stream and spring, and almost every sage bush behind which to hide. They would attack travelers or settlers, wagon trains, or whatever else offered itself as a target, both north and south of the Mexican border. They would disappear into the mountains and scatter, often ambushing their pursuers. The Apaches were a foe no less formidable than the Confederacy of Six Nations which at one time threatened the very existence of the newly founded American nation.

For some ten years Cochise and his small band held the army at bay and waged a bloody war throughout southern Arizona. In 1872 he finally surrendered and practically dictated the terms under which he would cease his activities. Tom Jeffords, who operated a stage line through the Cochise country and was a highly regarded friend of Cochise, was instrumental in arranging his surrender to General O. O. Howard.

The birth date of Cochise is not definitely known, but he died at Camp Bowie, Arizona, on June 8, 1874. He had been ill for several weeks.

Cochise did not engage in many parleys and his recorded speeches are few. This one is in the usual tone—that the Apache had done nothing but try to resist the white man and attempt to prevent him from taking over land rightfully belonging to the Indian. This talk was made by Cochise at a council which was held at the agency at Canada Alamosa, early in September of 1866. General Gordon Granger conducted the affairs of the council.

"You Must Speak Straight So That Your Words May Go As Sunlight to Our Hearts"

The sun has been very hot on my head and made me as in a fire; my blood was on fire, but now I have come into this valley and drunk of these waters and washed myself in them and they have cooled me. Now that I am cool I have come with my hands open to you to live in peace with you. I speak straight and do not wish to deceive or be deceived. I want a good, strong and lasting peace.

When God made the world he gave one part to the white man and another to the Apache. Why was it? Why did they come together? Now that I am to speak, the sun, the moon, the earth, the air, the waters, the birds and beasts, even the children unborn shall rejoice at my words. The white people have looked for me long. I am here! What do they want? They have looked for me long; why am I worth so much? If I am worth so much why not mark when I set my foot and look when I spit?

The coyotes go about at night to rob and kill; I can not see them; I am not God. I am no longer chief of all the Apaches. I am no longer rich; I am but a poor man. The world was not always this way. I can not command the animals; if I would they would not obey me. God made us not as you; we were born like the animals, in the dry grass, not on beds like you. This is why we do as the animals, go about of a night and rob and steal. If I had such things as you have, I would not do as I do, for then I would not need to do so. There are Indians who go about killing and robbing. I do not command them. If I did, they would not do so. My warriors have been killed in Sonora. I came here because God told me to do so. He said it was good to be at peace —so I came! I was going around the world with the clouds, and air, when God spoke to my thought and told me to come in here and be at peace with all. He said the world was for us all; how was it? When I was young I walked all over this country, east and west, and saw no other people than the Apaches. After many summers I walked again and found another race of people had come to take it. How is it? Why is it that the Apaches wait to die—that they carry their lives on their finger nails? They roam over the hills and plains and want the heavens to fall on them. The Apaches were once a great nation; they are now but few, and because of this they want to die and so carry their lives on the finger nails. Many have been killed in battle. You must speak straight so that your words may go as sunlight to our hearts. Tell me, if the Virgin Mary has walked throughout all the land, why has she never entered the wigwam of the Apache? Why have we never seen or heard her?

I have no father or mother; I am alone in the world. No one cares for Cochise; that is why I do not care to live, and wish the rocks to fall on me and cover me up. If I had a father and a mother like you, I would be with them and they with me. When I was going around the world, all were asking for Cochise. Now he is here—you see him and hear him—are you glad? If so, say so. Speak, Americans and Mexicans, I do not wish to hide anything from you nor have you hide anything from me; I will not lie to you; do not lie to me. I want to live in these mountains; I do not want to go to Tularosa. That is a long ways off. The flies on those mountains eat out the eyes of horses. The bad spirits live there. I have drunk of these waters and they have cooled me; I do not want to leave here.

Tall Bull, Cheyenne, birth date unknown; died July 11, 1869. This is a copy of a magnificent color portrait of Tall Bull painted by H. H. Cross in 1867.

Tall Bull

TALL BULL is a hereditary name among the Cheyenne Indians, and a number of the warriors were identified by this title. There are many members of the Cheyenne tribe who have Tall Bull as a surname at the present time. The Tall Bull considered here was a remarkable warrior, a strong and vigorous man, but little is known about when or where he was born, or in what part of the continent he ranged during his formative years.

Tall Bull's mother was a Sioux, and it was probable that his early years were spent on the Upper Plains. At any rate, he soon developed into the aggressive leader of a group of Cheyenne Dog Soldiers, and for some twenty years was a scourge on the plains of western Kansas, in Colorado, and up into the Sioux country in the Dakotas. His band consisted of about one hundred lodges, indicating approximately five hundred Indians under his leadership. Many of the Dog Soldiers had intermarried with the Sioux, and they were a wild and reckless band, daring and difficult to control.

Tall Bull was among the Cheyennes who attended the Medicine Lodge Treaty council in October of 1867. The noted George and Charles Bent, of Bent's Fort fame, were two of the interpreters for the Cheyennes. In spite of attending this big treaty, Tall Bull and his Dog Soldiers continued to harass the frontier settlers and travelers, and in 1869 they embarked upon a particularly savage series of raids along the Kansas-Colorado border. On July 11, 1869, a detachment of the Fifth Cavalry and a number of Pawnee scouts under the leadership of General E. A. Carr completely routed the Dog Soldiers at Summitt Springs, in Logan County, Colorado. Tall Bull was among those killed. Following the melee, one of the scouts "lifted" Tall

155

Bull's scalp, and it reputedly is now in the Pawnee Bill Museum in Pawnee, Oklahoma.

The following short speech by Tall Bull was in response to charges made by Major General W. S. Hancock on March 22, 1867, at a treaty session at Fort Leavenworth, Kansas, at which time Hancock charged Tall Bull with keeping white prisoners which he was reported to have taken. As usual, the injunction by the general was lengthy, and the reply of Tall Bull was terse and indicative of Indian desperation.

"You Sent for Us; We Came Here"

You sent for us; we came here. We have made the treaty with our agent, Colonel Wynkoop. We never did the white man any harm; we don't intend to. Our agent told us to meet you here. Whenever you want to go on the Smoky Hill you can go; you can go on any road. When we come on the road, your young men must not shoot us. We are willing to be friends with the white man.

This boy you have here—we have seen him; we don't recognize him; he may belong to some other tribe south of the Arkansas. The buffalo are diminishing fast. The antelope, that were plenty a few years ago, they are now thin. When they shall all die we shall be hungry; we shall want something to eat, and we will be compelled to come into the fort. Your young men must not fire at us; whenever they see us they fire, and we fire on them.

The Kiowas, Comanches, Apaches, and Arapahoes—send and get them here, and talk with them.

You say you are going to the village tomorrow. If you go, I shall have no more to say to you there than here. I have said all that I want to say. I don't know whether the Sioux are coming here or not. They did not tell me they were coming.

I have spoken.

Ten Bears, Comanche, born 1792; died October 23, 1872. From a
portrait made in Washington, D.C., in 1872.
COURTESY BUREAU OF AMERICAN ETHNOLOGY

Ten Bears

TEN BEARS was one of the most influential of the Comanche chieftains in the period immediately following the Civil War. He was the leading spokesman for the Comanches at the great Medicine Lodge council in 1867, and declared that he spoke for all the Comanches, and that they would do as he agreed they should. This was borne out by subsequent action of the Comanches, with the exception of the band led by young Quanah Parker, which continued its raiding.

Ten Bears took part in all council sessions affecting Southwestern Indians, and used his influence for peace. He was always interested in how the proposals made in council would affect his people. He was a very patriotic leader. In a council held in 1865, one of the peace commissioners said Ten Bears "is a fine old man, has been to Washington, and will use his influence for peace."

As head chief of the Yamperethka Comanches, he was sent to Washington for talks with the Great White Father. The trip, late in 1872, was a tiring experience for the old chief and he returned home weak and exhausted. Still he admonished his people to accept the white man's ways and live in peace, but his people spurned his advice. He died a disappointed old man.

Ten Bears was born about 1792, and died October 23, 1872, when he was about eighty years old.

The speech given here was made October 20, 1867, at the Medicine Lodge council, at which were assembled the greatest number of chiefs and warriors ever to be gathered at one place. Ten Bears was among the first of the Indians to address the peace commissioners. He assured them that he was the voice of the Comanches by

159

saying: "What I say is law for the Comanches, but it takes half a dozen to speak for the Kiowa."

Here is his speech.

"Do Not Ask Us to Give Up the Buffalo for the Sheep"

My heart is filled with joy, when I see you here, as the brooks fill with water, when the snows melt in the spring, and I feel glad, as the ponies do when the fresh grass starts in the beginning of the year. I heard of your coming, when I was many sleeps away, and I made but few camps before I met you. I knew that you had come to do good to me and to my people. I looked for the benefits, which would last forever, and so my face shines with joy, as I look upon you. My people have never first drawn a bow or fired a gun against the whites. There has been trouble on the line between us, and my young men have danced the war dance. But it was not begun by us.

It was you who sent out the first soldier, and it was we who sent out the second. Two years ago, I came up upon this road, following the buffalo, that my wives and children might have their cheeks plump, and their bodies warm. But the soldiers fired on us, and since that time there has been a noise, like that of a thunderstorm, and we have not known which way to go. So it was upon the Canadian. Nor have we been made to cry once alone. The blue-dressed soldiers and the Utes came from out of the night, when it was dark and still, and for campfires, they lit our lodges. Instead of hunting game, they killed my braves and the warriors of the tribe cut short their hair for the dead. So it was in Texas. They made sorrow come into our camps, and we went out like the buffalo bulls, when the cows are attacked. When we found them we killed them, and their scalps hang in our lodges.

The Comanches are not weak and blind, like the pups of a

160

dog when seven sleeps old. They are strong and farsighted, like grown horses. We took their road and we went on it. The white women cried, and our women laughed. But there are things which you have said to me which I do not like. They were not sweet like sugar, but bitter like gourds. You said that you wanted to put us upon a reservation, to build us houses and to make us Medicine lodges. I do not want them.

I was born upon the prairie, where the wind blew free, and there was nothing to break the light of the sun. I was born where there were no enclosures, and where everything drew a free breath. I want to die there, and not within walls. I know every stream and every wood between the Rio Grande and the Arkansas. I have hunted and lived over that country. I lived like my fathers before me, and like them, I lived happily.

When I was at Washington, the Great Father told me that all the Comanche land was ours, and that no one should hinder us in living upon it. So why do you ask us to leave the rivers, and the sun, and the wind, and live in houses? Do not ask us to give up the buffalo for the sheep. The young men have heard talk of this, and it has made them sad and angry. Do not speak of it more. I love to carry out the talk I get from the Great Father. When I get goods and presents, I and my people feel glad since it shows that he holds us in his eye. If the Texans had kept out of my country, there might have been peace. But that which you now say we must live on is too small.

The Texans have taken away the places where the grass grew the thickest and the timber was the best. Had we kept that, we might have done the thing you ask. But it is too late. The white man has the country which we loved and we only wish to wander on the prairie until we die. Any good thing you say to me shall not be forgotten. I shall carry it as near to my heart as my children, and it shall be as often on my tongue as the name of the

Great Spirit. I want no blood upon my land to stain the grass. I want it all clear and pure, and I wish it so, that all who go through among my people may find peace when they come in, and leave it when they go out.

Satank, Kiowa, born 1810; died June 8, 1871.

Satank

SATANK, Kiowa chief and medicine man, was born in the Black Hills region about 1810. He was considered to be an old man by Satanta, Lone Wolf, and Kicking Bird when they were leading the Kiowas on wide-ranging forays on the High Plains and in the Southwest. Some reports indicate that Satank was sixty-seven years old at the time of the Medicine Lodge Treaty. If this is true, his birth date would be about 1800. As is the case with many Indians, little definite information can be found to determine an accurate birth date.

Satank was the principal agent for peace in negotiations between the Kiowas and Cheyennes about 1840. He signed a peace treaty at Fort Atkinson, Kansas, in 1853, at a council which was attended by the Kiowas, Kiowa-Apaches, and Comanches.

The Kiowa calendar records that in the summer of 1864 Satank camped at Fort Larned, Kansas, where he shot a soldier. The fort's horses were stampeded and the Indians hastily abandoned their camp.

In 1867 he was present at the big council on Medicine Lodge Creek, and spoke before the largest group ever gathered for a council. In spite of the treaty, he led a raid into Texas on May 17, 1871, in which seven white men were killed. Later, bragging about this activity, he was arrested, tried, and convicted.

While being transported to prison in a wagon, he produced a knife which he had concealed in his breechcloth and slashed at a soldier guard. Satank was shot to death. Unable to face the prospect of imprisonment, he had chosen to die, and June 8, 1871, marked the end for this rugged warrior. He was buried in the military cemetery at Fort Sill, Oklahoma.

The following talk was made by Satank at Medicine Lodge, and was printed in the *New York Tribune* on November 30, 1867, as a communication from the peace commission camp on Medicine Lodge Creek. The story was dated October 23, 1867, and was written by a "special correspondent" who was in attendance at the council. There was about a four-week delay from the time the report was written until it appeared in print.

Note his claim that he observed the treaties. It may have been that the younger warriors would not honor the commitments that he tried to make for his tribe.

"Teach Us the Road to Travel, and We Will Not Depart from It Forever"

It has made me glad to meet you, who are the commissioners of the Great Father. You no doubt are tired of the much talk of our people. Many of them have put themselves forward and filled you with their sayings. I have kept back and said nothing, not that I did not consider myself still the principal chief of the Kiowa nation, but others, younger than I, desired to talk, and I left it to them. Before leaving, however, as I now intend to go, I come to say that the Kiowas and Comanches have made with you a peace, and they intend to keep it. If it brings prosperity to us, we, of course, will like it better. If it brings poverty and adversity we will not abandon it. It is our contract and it shall stand.

Our people once carried on war against Texas. We thought the Great Father would not be offended, for the Texans had gone out from among his people and become his enemies. You now tell us they have made peace and returned to the great family. The Kiowa and Comanche will now make no bloody trail in their land. They have pledged their word, and that word shall last unless the whites shall break their contract and invite the horrors of war.

We do not break treaties. We make but few contracts, and them we remember well. The whites make so many they are liable to forget them. The white chief seems not to be able to govern his braves. The Great Father seems powerless in the face of his children. He sometimes becomes angry when he sees the wrongs of his people committed on the red man, and his voice becomes loud as the roaring winds. But, like the wind, it soon dies away, and leaves the sullen calm of unheeded oppression. We hope now that a better time has come.

If all would talk and then do as you have done, the sun of peace would shine forever. We have warred against the white man, but never because it gave us pleasure. Before the day of oppression came, no white man came to our villages and went away hungry. It gave us more joy to share with him than it gave him to partake of our hospitality. In the far-distant past there was no suspicion among us. The world seemed large enough for both the red man and the white man. Its broad plains seem now to contract, and the white man grows jealous of his red brother. He once came to trade; he comes now to fight. He once came as a citizen; he now comes as a soldier. He once put his trust in our friendship, and wanted no shield but our fidelity, but now he builds forts and plants big guns on their walls. He once gave us arms and powder, and bade us hunt the game. We then loved him for his confidence. He now suspects our plighted faith, and drives us to be his enemies. He now covers his face with a cloud of jealousy and anger, and tells us to begone, as the offended master speaks to his dog.

We thank the Great Spirit that all these wrongs are now to cease, and the old day of peace and friendship to come again. You came as friends. You talked as friends. You have patiently heard our many complaints. To you they have seemed trifling; to us they are everything.

You have not tried, as many do, to get from us our lands for nothing. You have not tried to make a new bargain merely to get the advantage. You have not asked to make our annuities smaller; but, unasked, you have made them larger. You have not withdrawn a single gift, but voluntarily you have provided new guarantees for our education and comfort.

When we saw these things we then said, "These are the men of the past." We at once gave your our hearts. You now have them. You know what is best for us. Do for us what is best. Teach us the road to travel, and we will not depart from it forever. For your sakes the green grass shall not be stained with the blood of the whites. Your people shall again be our people, and peace shall be our mutual heritage. If wrong comes, we shall look to you for the right. We know you will not forsake us, and tell your people to be as you have been. I am old and will soon join my father, but those who come after me will remember this day. It is now treasured up by the old, and will be carried by them to the grave, and then handed down to be kept as a sacred tradition by their children and their children's children.

There is not a drop of my blood in the veins of any creature living, and when I am gone to the happy land, who will mourn for Satank? And now the time has come that I must go. Good by! You may never see me more, but remember Satank as the white man's friend!

Satanta, Kiowa, born about 1830; died October 11, 1878.

Satanta

SATANTA, one of the great Kiowa chieftains, has been called the "Orator of the Plains." He was tall and good looking, of commanding presence, and had a quick temper and sharp wit. He was noted for his love of talking, and some reports indicate he may have been more affected by his own speaking than were his listeners.

Satanta participated in several council meetings, the one of greatest significance being that held at Medicine Lodge Creek in 1867. He was a brave and aggressive leader on the warpath, and was not one to be left out of any raiding activity. Satanta protested about deplorable conditions of the Indians and talked about his love for peace, but Lawrie Tatum in his book *Our Red Brothers* says that instead of observing his promises not to raid, the Kiowa chief appeared to be leading his warriors on their forays.

Satanta, Lone Wolf, Kicking Bird, and Satank led the Kiowas on wide-ranging sweeps through the Plains area, striking quickly and disappearing into the open country on their swift ponies, carrying scalps and driving livestock ahead of them.

Satanta was born about 1830, and after a full career of raiding and warfare was sentenced to a term in the Texas state prison at Huntsville, Texas, where he committed suicide on October 11, 1878. He was buried in the prison cemetery, but his remains were exhumed and reburied at Fort Sill, Oklahoma, on June 23, 1963.

Satanta was at his best as an orator when he attended a council with Major General Winfield S. Hancock, who was commanding the Department of the Missouri. The council was held at Fort Larned, Kansas, on May 1, 1867.

This meeting was a preliminary to the Medicine Lodge council,

171

and efforts were made to meet with as many of the tribes of the area as possible.

The railroad Satanta refers to was the Union Pacific, which in 1867 had been built as far west as Fort Hayes, Kansas. Workers felt the wrath of the Indians, and were under almost constant attack. The Indians were united in their opposition to the railroad, and Cheyennes, Arapahoes, Kiowas, Comanches, Northern Cheyennes, Brulé and Ogalala Sioux, and Pawnees joined in the attacks. The wagon road was the Santa Fe Trail.

Henry M. Stanley in *My Early Travels and Adventures* records the speeches made by many Indians at these councils, but his reporting is somewhat different from the text of the speech given here. This version is taken from *Reports of Major General W. S. Hancock upon Indian Affairs, With Accompanying Exhibits.* Evidently the secretary recording the speech was better able to hear the translation of the speeches, and there is a significant difference in the wording.

The General Smith referred to by Satanta was Major General A. J. Smith, who was commanding the Seventh Cavalry which was stationed at Fort Dodge.

Hancock interrupted Satanta several times, but the speaker held on until he had completed what he wanted to say. Here is his speech:

"My Heart Is Very Strong"

I look upon you and General Smith as my fathers. I want friends, and I say, by the sun, and the earth I live on, I want to talk straight and tell the truth. All other tribes are my brothers, and I want friends, and am doing all I can for peace. If I die first, it is all right. All of the Indians south of here are my friends. When I first started out as a warrior I was a boy; now I am a man, and all men are my friends.

I want the Great Father at Washington, and all the soldiers and troops to hold on. I don't want the prairies and country to be bloody, but just hold on for a while. I don't want war at all; I want peace. As for the Kiowas talking war, I don't know anything about it. Nor do I know anything about the Comanches,

172

Cheyennes, and Sioux talking about war. The Cheyennes, Kiowas, and Comanches are poor. They are all of the same color.
They are all red men. This country here is old, and it all belongs
to them. But you are cutting off the timber, and now the country
is of no account at all. I don't mean anything bad by what I say.

I have nothing bad hidden in my breast at all; everything is
all right there. I have heard that there are many troops coming
out in this country to whip the Cheyennes, and that is the reason
we were afraid, and went away. The Cheyennes, Arapahoes,
and Kiowas heard that there were troops coming out in this
country; so also the Comanches and Apaches, but do not know
whether they were coming for peace or for war. They were on
the lookout, and listening, and hearing from down out of the
ground all the time. They were afraid to come in.

I don't think the Cheyennes wanted to fight, but I understand
you burned their village. I don't think that was good at all. To
you, General, and to all these officers sitting around here, I say
that I know that whatever I tell you will be sent to Washington,
and I don't want anything else but the truth told. Other chiefs
of the Kiowas, who rank below me, have come in to look for
rations, and to look about, and their remarks are reported to
Washington, but I don't think their hearts are good.

(Colonel Leavenworth said: What he means by that is, that
other chiefs make speeches for nothing but to get something
to eat.)

Satanta continued:

Lone Wolf, Stumbling Bear, and Kicking Bird all came in
with that object, and their speeches amount to nothing. The
Cheyennes, the Arapahoes, the Comanches, Kiowas, Apaches,
and some Sioux, all sent to see me, for they know me to be the
best man, and sent information that they wanted peace. They
do not work underhanded at all, but declare plainly that they
want peace. I hope that you two generals, and all these officers

173

around here, will help me, and give me heart, and help the Cheyennes, and not destroy them, but let them live. All of the Indians South of this desire the same, and when they talk that way to me I give them praise for it.

Whatever I hear in this council, and whatever you tell me, I will repeat when I reach my villages, and there are some Cheyennes over there whom I will tell, and will induce them to preserve peace. But if they will not listen to me, all my men and myself will have nothing more to do with them. I want peace, and will try to make them keep peaceful. The Kiowa braves have grown up from childhood, obtaining their medicine from the earth. Many have grown old, and continue growing old, and dying from time to time, but there are some remaining yet.

I do not want war at all, but want to make friends, and am doing the best I can for that purpose. There are four different bands of Comanches camped at different points in the south, along on the streams, and there are five different bands of Kiowas, those of Lone Wolf, Heap of Bears, Timber Mountain, Black Bird, and Stumbling Bear, and they profess to be chiefs, although they have but two or three lodges each. They are waiting, however, to hear what they can learn before taking the war path. The Kiowas do not say anything, and whatever the white man says is all right for them. The Kiowas and the white men are in council today, but I hope no mistake will be made about what the Indians say here, and that nothing will be added to it, because I know that everything is sent right to Washington.

(General Hancock: There are two or three interpreters here to witness, and prevent mistakes in the translation, so that it will be properly written down.)

Satanta continued:

About two o'clock I want to start back to Fort Dodge, and I want you to give me a letter.

(General Hancock: As soon as I can copy it I will give you

the written proceedings of this council, but cannot say that I can give it to you as soon as that.)

Satanta:

I simply want a letter when I go into camp, so that I can show it.

(General Hancock: I will give you a copy of the proceedings to take with you, so that you may show it to any man who may be able to read it to you.)

Satanta continued:

As for this Arkansas wagon road, I have no objection to it, but I don't want any railroad here, but upon the Smoky Hill route a railroad can run there, and it is all right. On the Arkansas and all those northern streams, there is no timber; it has all been cut off; but, nevertheless, if anybody knows of anything bad being done, I do not like it.

There are no longer any buffaloes around here, nor anything else we kill to live on; but I am striving for peace now, and don't want anything construed to be bad from what I say, because I am simply speaking the plain truth. The Kiowas are poor. Other tribes are very foolish. They make war and are unfortunate, and then call upon the Kiowas to aid them, and I don't know what to think about it. I want peace, and all these officers around this country know it. I have talked with them until now I am tired. I came down here, and brought my women with me, but came for peace.

If any white men steal our stock, I will report it openly. I continue to come often and am not tired. Now I am doing the best I can, and the white man is looking for me. If there were no troops in this country, and the citizens only lived around here, that would be better. But there are so many troops coming in here that I fear they will do something bad to me.

When Satank shot the sentinel here at the post, some two or three years since, there was then war, and that was bad. I came

175

near losing my life then. The Kiowas have now thrown him (Satank) away. If the Indians up north wish to act foolishly, that is not any of my business, and is no reason why we should do so down here. If the Indians further south see the white men coming, they will not come up on the war path, nor fight. They will not do so if they want to fight, but will call a council, to come and talk as they do here now. Today it is good and tonight it is good, and when the grass comes it will be good; and this road which runs up to the west is good also. Everything is all right now.

If you keep the horses herded around here close to the fort, they will never be good. Let them run away off on the prairies; there is no danger. Let them get grass, and they will get fat; but do not let the children and boys run away off on the hills now. That is not good. I don't do it, nor do the Cheyennes. I think that is a very good idea. You are a big chief, but when I am away over to the Kiowas, then I am a big chief myself.

Whenever a trader comes to my camp I treat him well, and do not do anything out of the way to him. All the traders are laughing and shaking hands with me. When the Indians get a little liquor they get drunk and fight sometimes, and sometimes they whip me; but when they get sober they are all right, and I don't think anything about it. All the white men around here can look at me, and hear what I say. I am doing all I can to keep my men down, and doing the best I can to have peace. Down at the mouth of the Little Arkansas, where a treaty was made, Colonel Leavenworth was present, and I was the first man who came in there to make peace with Colonel Leavenworth, and I did it all by my word.

Little Mountain, the former chief of the tribe, is now dead. He did all he could to make peace, and kept talking and talking, but the white man kept doing something bad to him, and he was in so much misery that he died. The white men and Indians kept fighting each other backward and forward, and then I came in and make peace myself. Little Mountain did not give me my commission. I won it myself. These three braves (pointing to some Indians around him) are chiefs also, and are not afraid of soldiers, and the sight of them does not frighten them at all. The prairie is large and good, and so are the heavens above, and I do not want them stained by the blood of war. I don't want you to trouble yourself and have fear about bringing out too many trains in this country, for I don't want to see any wagons broken or destroyed by war.

Now, I want to find out what is the reason Colonel Leavenworth did not give me some annuity goods. I have never talked bad, and I don't want to talk bad, but I want to find out the reason I did not get my annuity goods. There are Lone Bear, Heap of Bears, Stumbling Bear, and Little Heart, and others, six chiefs with very small bands, and they all received annuity goods, while those of my tribe are as plenty as the grass, and I came in for my goods and did not see them. You can look upon us all, and see if we have any of those goods. All that we have we have bought and paid for. We are all poor men; and I think others have got all the goods; but let them keep them. I want peace, and I don't want to make war on account of our goods. I expect to trade for what I get, and not get anything for making speeches.

My heart is very strong. We can make robes and trade them. That is what we live upon. I have no mules, horses, nor robes to give Colonel Leavenworth for my goods. I am a poor man, but I am not going to get angry and talk about it. I simply want to tell this to these officers here present. Such articles of clothing as the white man may throw away we will pick up and brush off and use, and make out the best we can; and, if you throw away provisions, we will clean and use them also, and thus do the best we can.

I see a great many officers around here with fine clothing, but I do not come to beg. I admire fine clothes, although I never did beg, or anything of that sort. I have no hat, and am going about without one, the same as all the other Kiowas. Colonel Bent used to come over often to my tent, and the Kiowas went there to him very often, and were glad and shook hands with him; and Mr. Curtis went there, and he was treated the same way. All were treated the same. But I am not poor enough to die yet. I think my women can make enough to live upon, and can make something yet.

When Colonel Bent was our agent, and brought our goods to us, he brought them out and kept them in a train; and when he arrived he unloaded all our goods to us, and that was the way to do it. But now there is a different way of doing things. At my camp I waited and sent for the agent, and did not see him; but other chiefs mounted their horses, and went there and claimed to be principal men.

I heard that the railroad was to come up through this country, and my men and other tribes objected to it; but I advised them to keep silent. I thought that by the railroad being built up through here, we would get our goods sure, but they do not come. I would like to get some agent who is a good and responsible man—one who would give us all our annuities. I do not want an agent who will steal half of our goods and hide them, but an agent who will get all my goods and bring them out here, and give them to me.

I am not talking any thing badly or angrily, but simply the truth. I don't think the great men at Washington know anything about this, but I am now telling your officers to find it out.

Now I am done and whatever you (General Hancock) have to say to me I will listen to, and those who are with me will listen, so that when we return to camp we can tell others the same as you tell us.

The next speech was delivered at the Medicine Lodge council held on Medicine Lodge Creek in Kansas, which was in progress October 19 and 20, 1867. Satanta was reluctant to speak before the treaty council, but finally rose to his feet and spoke. This speech was widely quoted, and the following version was taken from the *New York Times*, in which it was printed shortly after delivery.

There were some five thousand Indians gathered for the council, along with the peace commissioners, representatives of the press, traders, interpreters, guides, and others. Tribes represented at the council included the Comanches, Kiowas, Arapahoes, Cheyennes, and the Kiowa-Apaches.

The speech was delivered in Spanish.

"I Love the Land and the Buffalo and Will Not Part with It"

You, the commissioners, have come from afar to listen to our grievances. My heart is glad and I shall hide nothing from you. I understood that you were coming down to see us. I moved away from those disposed for war, and I also came along to see you. The Kiowas and Comanches have not been fighting. We were away down south when we heard you were coming to see us.

The Cheyennes are those who have been fighting with you. They did it in broad daylight so that all could see them. If I had been fighting I would have done it by day and not in the dark. Two years ago I made peace with Generals Harney, Sanborn and Colonel Leavenworth at the mouth of the Little Arkansas.

That peace I have never broken. When the grass was growing in the spring, a large body of soldiers came along on the Santa Fe road. I had not done anything and therefore I was not afraid. All the chiefs of the Kiowas, Comanches, and Arapahoes are here today; they have come to listen to good words. We have been waiting here a long time to see you and are getting tired. All the land south of the Arkansas belongs to the Kiowas and Comanches, and I don't want to give away any of it. I love the land and the buffalo and will not part with it. I want you to understand well what I say. Write it on paper. Let the Great Father see it, and let me hear what he has to say. I want you to understand, also, that the Kiowas and Comanches don't want to fight, and have not been fighting since we made the treaty. I hear a great deal of good talk from the gentlemen whom the Great Father sends us, but they never do what they say. I don't want any of the medicine lodges (schools and churches) within the country. I want the children raised as I was. When I make peace, it is a long and lasting one—there is no end to it. We thank you for your presents.

All the headmen and braves are happy. They will do what you want them, for they know you are doing the best you can. I and they will do our best also. When I look upon you, I know you are all big chiefs. While you are in this country we go to sleep happy and are not afraid. I have heard that you intend to settle us on a reservation near the mountains. I don't want to settle. I love to roam over the prairies. There I feel free and happy, but when we settle down we grow pale and die.

I have laid aside my lance, bow, and shield, and yet I feel safe in your presence. I have told you the truth. I have no little lies hid about me, but I don't know how it is with the commissioners. Are they as clear as I am?

A long time ago this land belonged to our fathers; but when I go up to the river I see camps of soldiers on its banks. These soldiers cut down my timber; they kill my buffalo; and when I see that, my heart feels like bursting; I feel sorry. I have spoken.

Gall, Sioux, born about 1840; died December 5, 1894.

Gall

GALL was one of the greatest of the Hunkpapa Sioux chieftains, and some historians consider him to be the peer of the famous Red Cloud and of Spotted Tail. Gall was one of the leaders of the Hunkpapa Sioux during the time of the fabulous Sitting Bull.

Gall was a superb specimen of manhood, rugged and able. On one occasion he had stolen some ponies and a detachment of a hundred soldiers was sent to his village to arrest him. The soldiers surrounded the village at about 2 A.M., announcing that they wanted Gall. He was aroused, stuck his head out of his tipi, and was promptly shot at by one of the soldiers.

Gall dashed to the back of the tipi, slashed a hole, and started to leap out. Soldiers, armed with rifles and bayonets, were all around, and slammed him to the ground. They clubbed, stomped, and stabbed him, and one soldier had to put his foot on Gall's body to retrieve his bayonet. Thinking Gall dead, they left him lying in the snow.

Other Indians in the camp would not touch his body, and they quickly moved their tipis to another location. Gall later revived, and in spite of his terrible wounds and the fact that he was nearly naked in the cold and snow, made his way to the lodge of a friend some twenty miles away. The friend cared for him until he recovered from his ordeal, but one of the wounds remained open for more than a year.

After this affair, Gall carried a lasting hatred for the whites, and finally died December 5, 1894, as a result of his horrible wounds. His birth has been recorded as c. 1840.

His speech here is brief and was made at Fort Rice in 1868 at a peace conference which was headed by General "White Beard"

183

Harney, General Alfred H. Terry, and General John B. Sanborn.

Basis for the story of the brutal treatment and recovery of Gall is Stanley Vestal's book *New Sources of Indian History, 1850–1891*, which states that Gall was camped at the time near Fort Berthold, where he went to trade. Stanley Vestal was the pseudonym for Walter S. Campbell, a prolific writer on Western and Indian subjects. He wrote that "some time after" the Treaty of Laramie at Fort Rice in 1868 the incident took place. No definite date can be found.

Vestal spent many months among the Sioux gathering material for his fine book on Sitting Bull, and he knew many of the old Indians. Few white men gained the confidence of the Sioux as well as did Vestal. The author was fortunate to hear Vestal (Campbell) tell some of his experiences among the Sioux and during his childhood in Oklahoma.

Vestal had great amounts of material that could not be used in his book on Sitting Bull, and this incident about Gall must have been some of the "leftover" that could not be ignored.

"If We Make Peace, You Will Not Hold It"

God raised me with one thing only, and I keep that yet. There is one thing that I do not like. The whites ruin our country. If we make peace, the military posts on this Missouri River must be removed and the steamboats stopped from coming up here. Below here is the Running Water, which is our country. You fought me and I had to fight back: I am a soldier. The annuities you speak of we don't want. Our intention is to take no present.

You talk of peace. If we make peace, you will not hold it. We told the good Black Robe (De Smet) who has been to our camp that we do not like these things. I have been sent here by my people to see and hear what you have got to say. My people told me to get powder and ball, and I want that.

Now, many things have happened that are not our fault. We are blamed for many things. I have been stabbed. If you want to make peace with me, you must remove this Fort Rice, and

184

stop the steamboats. If you won't, I must get all these friendly (Agency) Indians to move away. I have told all this to them, and now I tell you.

Red Cloud, Sioux, born about 1822; died December 10, 1909. This portrait was made about 1875.

Red Cloud

RED CLOUD was one of the most powerful of the Sioux Indian chieftains. He was born in 1822 in the area between the Black Hills and the Missouri River, and developed into a strong, virile, and fearless leader. He had a record of more than eighty individual feats of courage to count in his deeds of war and valor. Red Cloud commanded the war party at the Fetterman Massacre in December, 1866, and at the Wagon Box Fight in August, 1867. His group attacked the Hayfield Party near Fort C. F. Smith.

Red Cloud was in a group of Indians which went to Washington in 1870, and his actions and speech indicated that he had changed his ideas about war and was an advocate of peace. His trip was called Red Cloud's Peace Crusade. He was a guest of President Ulysses S. Grant in the White House, and then went to New York, where on June 16 he made an address at the Cooper Institute, appearing before a capacity audience.

In reporting the speech, a front page story in the *New York Times* of June 17, 1870, commented:

No one who listened to Red Cloud's remarkable speech yesterday can doubt that he is a man of very great talents. . . . He has spent his life fighting the battles of his people, and one day he is transplanted to Cooper Institute, and asked to put on a clean shirt, a new waistcoat, a high crowned hat, and then make a speech. . . . His earnest manner, his impassioned gestures, the eloquence of his hands, and the magnetism which he evidently exercises over his audience, produced a vast effect on the dense throng which listened to him yesterday. "You have children, and so have we. We want to rear our children well, and ask you to help us in doing so." It seems to us that this is not an unreasonable request even though it does come from a "savage."

187

Red Cloud liked to say, "The President is a friend of mine." He aged rapidly while living on the reservation, and became blind and decrepit. He died December 10, 1909.

"I Represent the Whole Sioux Nation, and They Will Be Bound by What I Say"

My brothers and my friends who are before me today. God Almighty has made us all, and He is here to hear what I have to say to you today. The Great Spirit made us both. He gave us land, and he gave you land. You came here and we received you as brothers. When the Almighty made you, He made you all white and clothed you. When He made us, He made us with red skins and poor. When you first came we were very many and you were few. You do not know who appears before you to speak. He is a representative of the original American race, the first people on this continent. We are good, and not bad. The reports which you get about us are all on one side. You hear of us only as murderers and thieves. We are not so. If we had more lands to give you, we would give them, but we have no more. We are driven into a very little island, and we want you, our dear friends, to help us with the Government of the United States.

The Great Spirit made us poor and ignorant. He made you rich and wise and skillful in things which we know nothing about. The good Father made you to eat tame game, and us to eat wild game. Ask any one who has gone through to California. They will tell you we have treated them well. You have children. We, too, have children, and we wish to bring them up well. We ask you to help us do it.

At the mouth of Horse Creek, in 1852, the Great Father made a treaty with us. We agreed to let him pass through our territory unharmed for fifty-five years. We kept our word. We committed no murders, no depredations, until the troops came there. When the troops were sent there trouble and disturbance arose. Since that time there have been various goods sent from time to time to us, but only once did they reach us, and soon the Great Father took away the only good man he had sent to us, Colonel Fitzpatrick. The Great Father said we must go to farming, and some of our men went to farming near Fort Laramie, and we were treated very badly indeed.

We came to Washington to see our Great Father that peace might be continued. The Great Father that made us both wishes peace to be kept; we want to keep peace. Will you help us? In 1868 men came out and brought papers. We could not read them, and they did not tell us what was in them. We thought the treaty was to remove the forts, and that we should then cease from fighting. But they wanted to send us traders on the Missouri. We did not want to go to the Missouri, but wanted traders where we were. When I reach Washington, the Great Father explained to me what the treaty was, and showed me that the interpreters had deceived me. All I want is right and justice. I have tried to get from the Great Father what is right and just. I have not altogether succeeded. I want you to help me get what is right and just. I represent the whole Sioux nation, and they will be bound by what I say. I am no Spotted Tail, to say one thing one day and be bought for a pin the next. Look at me, I am poor and naked, but I am the Chief of the nation. We do not want riches but we do want to train our children right. Riches would do us no good. We could not take them with us to the other world. We do not want riches, we want peace and love.

The riches that we have in this world, Secretary Cox said truly, we cannot take with us to the next world. Then I wish to know why commissioners are sent out to us who do nothing but rob us and get the riches of this world away from us? I was brought up among the traders and those who came out there

189

in the early times treated me well and I had a good time with them. They taught us to wear clothes and to use tobacco and ammunition. But, by and by, the Great Father sent out a different kind of men; men who cheated and drank whiskey; men who were so bad that the Great Father could not keep them at home and so sent them out there.

I have sent a great many words to the Great Father but they never reached him. They were drowned on the way, and I was afraid the words I spoke lately to the Great Father would not reach you, so I came to speak to you myself; and now I am going away to my home. I want to have men sent out to my people whom we know and can trust. I am glad I have come here. You belong in the East, and I belong in the West, and I am glad I have come here and that we understand one another. I am very much obliged to you for listening to me. I go home this afternoon. I hope you will think of what I have said to you. I bid you all an affectionate farewell.

Blackfoot, Crow, born about 1795; died in fall of 1877. This portrait was taken in 1871 on Old Crow Indian Agency on Yellowstone River, near the Shields River.

Blackfoot

CHIEF BLACKFOOT'S place and date of birth are not known, and little has been learned of his childhood. He was a member of the Mountain Crow Tribe, which made its home in the territory around the Yellowstone headwaters.

Blackfoot became chief of the Crow Tribe in the 1850s. By the mid 1860s he had become head chief of the Mountain Crows. He represented the tribe at the important Fort Laramie Treaty in 1868. He was active in tribal affairs and took part in many council meetings, as well as the treaty held at the Crow Agency in Montana in 1873.

Blackfoot was a fine physical specimen, and was noted for his long harangues and his eloquence when in treaty and council meetings.

When well into his eighties he developed pneumonia and died near the present town of Meeteetse, Wyoming, in the fall of 1877. His wife had died from the same illness on the previous day. Both Blackfoot and his wife were buried in a cave.

The occasion for the first speech included here was at a council held at the Crow Agency in Montana, on August 11, 1873. Felix R. Brunot, chairman of the Board of Indian Commissioners, conducted the conference. The greater part of the recorded proceedings of the conference gives speeches by the whites, but true to his reputation, Blackfoot took advantage of the occasion and was able to make several speeches. In this talk he reveals the fears of the Indians that the flood of whites would increase and crowd his people, the fact that his young men were difficult to control, and his own fears for the future.

"May the White Man and the Indian Speak Truth to Each Other Today"

You call the Great Spirit Jesus in your language; we call him in the Crow language E-so-we-wat-se. I am going to light the pipe and talk to the Great Spirit. (He lighted the pipe, and, looking up reverently, said:) The Great Spirit has made the red man and the white man, and sees all before Him today. Have pity upon us! May the white man and the Indian speak truth to each other today. The sun that looks down upon us today, and gives us light and heat, sees that our hearts are true, and that what we do is good for the poor red man. The moon, that shines on us in the night time, will see us prosper and do well. The earth, on which we walk, from which we come, and which we love as our mother—which we love as our country— we ask thee to see that we do that which is good for us and our children. This tobacco comes from the whites; we mix it with bark from the Indian trees and burn it together before Thee, O Great Spirit! So may our hearts and the hearts of the white men go out together to Thee and be made good and right. (Blackfoot then got into his speech after passing the pipe around the council members.)

I am going to have a long talk with you. My Great Father sent our friends to see us. We see each other; that is good. You came here last summer; we were sent for to see you. We were back in the mountains when we heard of you, but high waters and the mountains prevented our coming. You said you did not see us, and you were sorry for it. We could not come any faster. This summer we were on this side, near the Yellowstone, where we were getting skins to make lodges. In the fall the traders will want our robes. We will then go over the Yellowstone to Judith's Basin to hunt. Since I was a boy I recollect that is what the Crows always did. When the Crows meet a friend they always give him something; so we do with you. You say you have a book that tells about the Great Spirit. We always give the Great Spirit something. I think that is good. We see the sun, we give him something; and the moon and the earth, we give them something. We beg them to take pity on us. The sun and moon look at us, and the ground gives us food. You come and see us, and that is why we give you something. We are men like each other; our religion is different from yours.

The old folks are dying off; then who will own the land? I went to Fort Laramie; the old Indians signed the treaty. We came back to the camp and told the young men, and they said we had done wrong and they did not want to have anything to do with it. They said, "We love the Great Father, and hold on to the hands of our white friend. All the other Indian tribes fight the whites; we do not do so. We love the whites, and we want them to leave us a big country."

All the other Indians go and talk with the Great Father; you take them to Washington; they are bad; they hide their hearts; but they talk good to the Great Father, and you do more for them than for us. This I want to tell you; yesterday you spoke to us and we listened to you. If you wish to have peace with all the Indians get them all together and make peace with them. Then I will make peace with them, too.

The Great Spirit made these mountains and rivers for us, and all this land. We were told so, and when we go down the river hunting for food we come back here again. We cross over to the other river, and we think it is good. Many years ago the buffalo got sick and died, and Mr. Maldron gave us annuity goods, and since then they have given us something every year. The guns you gave us we do not point at the whites. We do not shoot our white friends. We are true when we look you in the face. On our hands is no white man's blood. When you give us arms to go and fight the Sioux we fight them to keep our lands from them. When we raise our camp and go for buffalo some white men go with us; they see what we are doing; they see that we jump over the places that are bloody. On the other side of the river below, there are plenty of buffalo; on the mountains are plenty of elk and black-tail deer; and white-tail deer are plenty at the foot of the mountain. All the streams are full of beaver. In the Yellowstone River the whites catch trout; there are plenty of them. The white men give us food; we know nothing about it. Do not be in a hurry; when we are poor, we will tell you of it.

At Laramie we went to see the commissioners. Now commissioners come to see us, and we listen to what you say. The commissioners told us at Laramie if we remained good friends of the whites we would be taken care of for forty years. Since we made that treaty it is only five years. You are in a hurry to quit giving us food. I am a young man yet; my teeth are all good. They told us at Laramie we would get food till we were old, and our children after us.

This is not the place for the agency, on this point of rocks. We would like to know who built the agency here. They told us they would give us food. They promised to send a good agent and traders, and if they were not good they would be taken away. Pease never treated us wrong; the young men and the children he always treated right; all that was sent for us he gave us; he was not a thief; he treated us well, and we do not want him to go away from us.

On Sheep Mountain white men come; they are my friends; they marry Crow women, they have children with them; the men talk Crow. When we come from hunting we get off at their doors, and they give us something to eat. We like it. We raised Shane (the interpreter); he was a boy when he came here. You ask us what we have to say, and that is what we tell you. Here is the doctor; when our people are sick he doctors them. He has two children by a Crow woman; we like him. Here are our traders; when we go hunting they give us ammunition; they gave me a revolver to kill buffalo. We do not know anything about Cross (a new trader); we do not know his face. We want the soldiers at Ellis to take the part of the Crows. When they come here to see the giving of annuity goods we give them robes to take with them, and when they hear bad talk about the Crows we want them to speak well of us. When we camp here some of the whites run off with our horses into the mountains. We know about it, but we do not say anything. We have a strong heart, as firm as a rock, and we say nothing about it, but you want to hear what we have to say and I tell you. In Gallatin Valley the Cheyennes, Arapahoes, and Sioux made a raid and the people blamed the Crows with it. We want them to quit speaking bad about us. On the Missouri River the whites have married into all the different Indian tribes; their brothers-in-law, the white men, come here and steal our horses. We follow them and find who have them. Some of the Crows went to the Missouri River and got some Crow horses. The white people sent word they were their horses, and we sent them all back. We claim our horses, but they are not brought back.

When we set up our lodge-poles, one reaches to the Yellowstone; the other is on White River; another one goes to Wind River; the other lodges on the Bridger Mountains. This is our land, and so we told the commissioners at Fort Laramie; but all kinds of white people come over it, and we tell you of it, though we say nothing to them. On this side of the Yellowstone there is a lake; about it are buffalo. It is a rich country; the whites are on it; they are stealing our quartz; it is ours, but we say nothing to them. The whites steal a great deal of our money. We do not want them to go into our country. We would like needle-guns to get game and fight the Sioux; this we tell you.

The second speech by Blackfoot was delivered at the same treaty council on August 15. In it Blackfoot outlined the territory which his people claimed and dominated. He challenged the treaty commissioners to make a definite statement and give guarantees of what the government would do if the Crows would sell their land. He also indicated that the Indians were not unaware of the mineral wealth of the area, and he was concerned about the threats other tribes presented to the peace and welfare of the Crows.

"The Whites Think We Don't Know about the Mines, But We Do"

On this side of the river and on the other side is our country. If you do not know anything about it, I will tell you about it, for I was raised here. You mark all our country, the streams and mountains, and I would like to tell you about it; and what I say I want you to take to your heart. You make us think a great deal today. I am a man, and am talking to you. All the Indian tribes have not strong arms and brave hearts like we have; they are not so brave. We love you and shake hands with you (at this point he shook hands with Commissioner Brunot). We have gone to Judith Basin a great deal, and you wish us to take it for a reservation. All kinds of men go there; trappers and hunters go there poisoning game. The Sioux Indians, Crees, Santees, Mandans, Assineboines, Gros Ventres, Piegans, Pen d'Oreilles, Flatheads, the Mountain Crows, the River Crows, Bannacks, Snakes, and Nez Perc Indians and white people, all go there. You wish us to take the Judith Basin for a reservation. All these Indians will come, and we will likely quarrel; that is what we think about it.

Judith Basin is a small basin; a great many people go there; we all go there to eat buffalo. I have told you about the Sioux when they come to fight us. We go a long way from our camp. All Indians are not as strong as we are; they give up and run off. If you have two dogs, if they go to fight, and you catch them and pull them apart, when you let them go they fight again. So it is with the Sioux and Crows.

You tell me the railroad is coming up the Yellowstone. If you move this place away from here, the Sioux will be like a whirlwind; they will come and fight the whites; that is true as I tell you. Along Prior Mountain is the Crow Trail. We listen to you, and what I tell you is true. The young men do not care what they do. We want some of them to go to Washington with Major Pease (agent for the Crows), and what they say there will be all right. I will tell you what we will do; neither of us will live forever; in time both of us will die. We will sell the part of our reservation containing the mountains from Clark's Fork, below the mountains, and the valleys we will not sell. The Crow young men will go to Washington and fix it up, and come back and tell us about it. We will sell the range of mountains to Heart's Mountain and Clark's Ford. The young men will sell it at Washington, and they will say to the Great Father at Washington, that the Crows have a strong heart and are willing to sell their land. When you buy this and give us plenty for it, we will talk about the rest, if you want to buy it.

Those mountains are full of mines. The whites think we don't know about the mines, but we do. We will sell you a big country, all the mountains. Now tell us what you are going to give for our mountains. We want plenty for them. Am I talking right? The young men think I am talking right. Every one here is trying to get plenty. The railroad is coming. It is not here yet. You talk about Judith Basin. I have heard about it. I want to see what you will give for the mountains; then we will talk about the rest of our land. You think you have peace with the Sioux; I do not think you have. You want to shake hands with them. We want to know whether you are going to fight the Sioux or not; we want to know. We will see what the young men will do at Washington; if they hear what is good, we will do it. The railroad will not be here for some time, and before that we will be part of the time on this side and part of the time on the other side of the river. In the Gallatin Valley, if you sell a house and a little piece of ground, you get paid for it. I know that is the white man's way of doing. The white men are all around us. On the other side of the river all those streams belong to the Crows. When the Sioux come there, we can run them off into the river. We are friends; when our friends get horses stolen, we give them some. Many of our horses are stolen here; four of my horses are gone now; last night some horses were stolen. The Sioux took them along the mountains. On the other side of the gap, there are plenty of houses full of everything. In Gallatin Valley are plenty of cartridges; the Crows have none. If the Sioux come, I do not know what we shall fight them with.

See all these old women! They have no clothing; the young men have no good blankets. We would like the Nez Perces, when they raise camp, to come here; they die with the Crows; they help to fight the Sioux. The last commission told us we could eat buffalo a long time. While we are here, the Flathead Indians take our horses. I would like you to take our part and stop them.

At the end of his talk, Mr. Brunot told Blackfoot that they had talked about horses that morning, and Blackfoot expressed a wish for the commissioner in effect to "do something."

Kicking Bird, Kiowa, born about 1830; died May 5, 1875. Photograph made at Fort Dodge, Kansas, in 1868.

Kicking Bird

KICKING BIRD was a grandson of a Crow captive who was adopted into the Kiowa tribe. Early in life he made a place for himself in tribal affairs by his superior mental abilities. He was a leader in tribal functions, and also achieved fame as a warrior.

Kicking Bird had the wisdom to foresee that resistance to the whites was useless, and used his influence to persuade the tribe to accept conditions as they were. He was the first chief to sign an agreement to accept reservation status, on August 15, 1865, at a council near Wichita, Kansas. He was also a leading participant in the big Medicine Lodge council in 1867, which located the Kiowa-Comanche-Apache reservation in the Fort Sill area of Oklahoma. He was considered to be head chief of the Kiowas from 1874. Being seriously concerned with the future of his Indians, Kicking Bird invited the establishment of the first school on the reservation in 1873. One white observer said that if Kicking Bird had been white he could easily have been a United States senator.

Following his continued efforts to get the Kiowas to become more peaceful he became the subject of contempt from some of his tribesmen. Some opposition was intense, and when he died suddenly on May 5, 1875, it was suspected that he had been poisoned by his enemies. He was about forty years old. His family requested that he be buried with Christian rites.

Kicking Bird was one of the Indians who met for a council with Major General W. S. Hancock near Fort Dodge, on April 23, 1867, before the big Medicine Lodge council, which did not meet until October of that year. In explaining to the Indians the reason for the council, General Hancock said that he was trying to see what problems the Indians had, and attempt to ease them, as he was preparing for a big campaign to the north and west.

Kicking Bird, in his turn, told where his tribe was camped and assured the general he would work for peace.

"This Country South of the Arkansas Is Our Country"

I know you are a big chief. I heard some time ago that you were coming, and am glad to see you, and glad that you have taken us by the hand. Our great chief, Te-haw-son, is dead. He was a great chief for the whites and Indians. Whatever Te-haw-son said they kept in their hearts. Whatever Te-haw-son told them in council they remembered, and they would go the road he told them; that is, to be friendly to the whites. Te-haw-son always advised the nation to take the white man by the hand, and clear above the elbow. Kicking Bird advises the same.

We live south of the river. Kiowas, Comanches, Arapahoes, and Apaches, we all in our hearts want peace with the whites. This country south of the Arkansas is our country. We want peace in it, and not war. We have seen you, (General Hancock) and our hearts are glad. We will report the talk you have had with us to all of the nations, so that they will know what you have said. When there is no war south of the Arkansas, our women and children can sleep without fear of being molested, and our men can hunt buffalo there without fear of enemies. My heart is big and glad that you have told us that you will not make war on Indians whose consciences are good. We have often wished for the Sioux and Northern Cheyennes not to come down here. They steal our horses when they come here, and we do not want them to come.

I have heard that our goods are coming early this spring. When they arrive that will be the time to pick out young men for guides and scouts. After I get back to my people, I will tell the words you have said to our chiefs, and when it has been told our young men will report what they will do. You can see for yourself that we are peaceably encamped on the other side of the river, and no matter what kind of a storm came, we have staid to have a talk with you. Whatever you have to tell we will listen to, and we know that it is the truth. Now and then we have robes to trade for sugar and coffee for our women and children. On the prairie we eat buffalo meat. We are encamped close by here.

The following talk, made at a council with the Indian agent and other chiefs in the spring of 1873, found Kicking Bird feeling that he had been rejected after the agent made a statement in which he tried to build the ego and good will of another chief, Big Bow. This was not the case, however, and his white friends tried to reassure him after his talk. He did resume his efforts in the interest of peace.

"I Have Worked Hard to Bring My People on the White Man's Road"

I long ago took the white man by the hand; I have never let it go; I have held it with a strong and firm grasp. I have worked hard to bring my people on the white man's road. Sometimes I have been compelled to work with my back towards the white people so that they have not seen my face, and they may have thought I was working against them; but I have worked with one heart and one object. I have looked ahead to the future, and have worked for the children of my people, to bring them into a position that, when they became men and women, they will take up the white road. I have but two children of my own, but have worked for the children of my people as though they had all been mine. Five years I have striven for this thing, and all these years Big Bow worked against me to keep my people on the old bad road. When I brought in and delivered up white captives to the agent, Big Bow has taken more. Now for a little while he comes on to the good road. The agent has taken him by the hand, and thrown me away after my many years' labor.

I am as a stone, broken and thrown away—one part thrown this way, and one part thrown that way. I am a chief no more; but that is not what grieves me—I am grieved at the ruin of my people: they will go back to the old road, and I must follow them; they will not let me live with the white people. I shall go to my camp, and after a while I shall go a little farther, and then a little farther, until I get as far away as is possible for me. When they show me the big chief they select, I shall follow him wherever he leads. When you take hold of my hand today you have taken it for the last time; when you see me ride away today, you will see Kicking Bird no more. I shall never come back to this place.

Captain Jack, Modoc, born about 1837; died October 3, 1873.

Captain Jack

CAPTAIN JACK and his small band of Modoc Indians wrote a bloody story of resistance to oppression from the whites in the territory included in Northern California along the Oregon border. There were only some four or five hundred members of the Modoc tribe, but their small numbers gave little trouble until they became involved in the difficulties of neighboring tribes in their resistance to the whites.

The notorious Ben Wright had organized a party for the purpose of hunting Indians for the scalps, had mercilessly eradicated all he could locate, and had exhibited their scalps. The Indians fought back with such ferocity that the militia was called out to subdue them.

Captain Jack, born about 1837, was a leader of the Modocs, though he had trouble maintaining his position among warriors of the tribe. Finally at a peace conference, he and other members of the tribe killed three members of the commission, Jack being charged with the murder of General E. R. S. Canby. The Indians fled to the Lava Beds in the vicinity of Rhett (Modoc or Tule) Lake. This rugged country gave good protection to the Indians, and the military waged a costly and frustrating campaign before they were dislodged.

On June 1, 1873, Jack surrendered his group. The military force which had been trying to bottle him up consisted of 985 regulars and 71 Indians. Jack had 80 warriors at the start—which was cut down to 50—along with 120 women and children. Captain Jack was tried before a military court at Fort Klamath on July 5, 1873, and was sentenced to be hanged on October 3, 1873.

The speech here was made by Captain Jack on March 6, 1873, while efforts were being made to prevent open warfare.

The peace commission to the Modocs was headed by A. B. Meacham as chairman. Meacham had wide experience in Indian affairs, and wrote extensively of his experiences while doing this work. H. R. Clum was acting commissioner of Indian affairs in Washington.

Meacham recorded the speech of Captain Jack, with an explanation that Captain Jack's sister, Mary, was the intermediary who delivered the speech to him.

"I Have Said Yes, and Thrown Away My Country"

I am very sad. I want peace quick, or else let the soldiers come and make haste and fight. I want to stay here a little while, so that my people can get ready to go. I say yes to going to a warmer country; and this is the first time I have said yes. I don't want my people shot. I don't want my men to go with guns any more. I have quit forever. I have buried the past, and don't want to be mad for the past. I have heard they wanted to shoot me; that would be like shooting an old woman. I want to talk good words only. I don't want to shoot or be shot. I don't want any one to get mad as quick as they did before. I want to live in peace.

I want to go and see my people on the reservation. My mind is made up to say "yes." I have a good heart, and want no mistake made this time, to live with good heart and talk truth. I have no paper men, and can't write on paper. The papers called me bad and lied about me. If they don't lie to me, I won't lie to them. I want to give up shooting. I never have been out since I came on here. If they had come I would have shot them. I never have seen any white men except those who come here. I want Fairchild and Riddle and any one else willing to come out. I want to see my people at Yainax.

I have thrown away my country, and unless I go I never

210

expect to see my people again, and then I want to go to town, and then I will go away and never expect to return. I want to see what they have to say. My mind is made up, and I have but little else to say. They have got my heart now, and they must look after it and do right. I am nearly well and have a good heart now. I expect Mr. Meacham is very sick and couldn't come. I am nearly well; but I am afraid on account of the soldiers on the road. There are so many soldiers around. There are soldiers on Lost River, on Clear Lake, and Bernard's soldiers.

Wouldn't they be afraid if they were in the same situation? I want to see their head-men who never have been here. I have heard of so many soldiers coming I was afraid. When they visited me they laid down and slept and were not pestered. I had a bad heart when Mr. Steele left here yesterday morning, to think that he would not come back or believe me. If I know the new country I would go out when he came in. I want to visit my people, then the new country, and want the peace commission to go with me and show it to me.

I wish to live like the whites. Let everything be wiped out, washed out, and let there be no more blood. I have got a bad heart about those murderers. I have got but a few men and I don't see how I can give them up. Will they give up their people who murdered my people while they were asleep? I never asked for the people who murdered my people. I only talked that way.

I can see how I could give up my horse to be hanged; but I can't see how I could give up my men to be hanged. I could give up my horse to be hanged, and wouldn't cry about it; but if I gave up my men I would have to cry about it. I want them all to have good hearts now. I have thrown away everything. There must be no more bad talk. I will not. I have spoken forever. I want soldiers all to go home. I have given up now and want no more fuss. I have said yes, and thrown away my country.

I want soldiers to go away, so I will not be afraid. When I

go to Yainax I don't want to come back here; but want to go to town and then to the new country. I wanted to go to a new country and not come back any more to see my people; that is why I wanted to go to Yainax. I want to see how many of my relations would go with me.

I feel bad for my people in the lava beds. I would cry if I didn't see my people at Yainax. I don't know the new country, and they wouldn't know where they were. I know no country but Shasta and Pitt River. But I say yes, and consent to everything and go away. I don't want to live here any more, because I can't live here any more in peace. I wish to go to southern country and live in peace.

I want my people to stay here till I and some of my head men go and look at new country. I want Riddle and some others to go with me. I want clothing and food for my men. I want it given them here. I don't want them to think I am deceiving them. I want my people to be taken care of while I am looking for new country. I want to know where they can stay and eat at while I am gone. I want to stop with Fairchild.

I want to know if they got at me so quick because I couldn't believe them at once. I couldn't come; I had but two horses, and the Klamaths took my good one. I have no saddle, and my horses have been ridden so much they are not fit to ride. I am a chief; am proud; am ashamed to ride a poor horse.

I understand their talk now. It seems now that I had been with them and talked with them and seen them. I talk with my mouth. They have paper men to write down what I say. I want Fairchild[1] to come tomorrow to see me. Mary has brought back good news. I want to see them as bad as they want to see me. I don't want Fairchild to be afraid to come out with Mary. I want and hope Mary will come back with message and say yes, just as I have said.

1 The Fairchild referred to was John Fairchild, a rancher; Riddle was Frank Riddle, who was married to an Indian woman and was interpreter for the Modocs.

Crazy Horse, Sioux, born 1849; died September 5, 1877. While no really authentic picture of Crazy Horse exists, this photograph from the Rose Collection is said to be a picture of him. It was made by Major Wilhelm of the 8th U.S. Infantry in 1874, and is offered as the typical appearance of a Sioux chief at the time.

Crazy Horse

CRAZY HORSE, the greatest military genius of the Sioux Confederation, was born in 1849. Crazy Horse first came to the notice of writers about 1875, but the name was an old one, and was handed down from generation to generation. His family was highly regarded by the Indians, and had been entrusted with the Sioux history, which was portrayed on buckskin, for some eight hundred years. The buckskin was destroyed by fire many years ago.

Crazy Horse was an imposing figure, about six feet tall. He married a Cheyenne woman, and this resulted in close ties between his band of the Sioux and the Cheyennes. He was also a son-in-law of the famous Red Cloud.

Crazy Horse played an important part in the affairs of the Sioux, and was fearless in battle. He had a superstitious belief that he could not be killed by a bullet, and was disdainful of gunfire. He had lost two close friends and apparently had little desire to live. He is supposed to have told friends he was looking for death.

Indian police suspected that Crazy Horse might be planning an outbreak, and on September 5, 1877, a group of forty-three policemen were sent to arrest him. In the scuffle following the attempt to arrest Crazy Horse, a bayonet was run through his stomach. With police clinging to his arms and his friends trying to help him, Crazy Horse said: "Let me go, my friends, you have hurt me enough." At ten o'clock that night he called Indian Agent Jesse M. Lee to his side and spoke to him, shortly after which he died.

His superstition that he would not be killed by gunfire was good to the last—it was a bayonet thrust which ended his life. He was secretly buried by his parents somewhere in the hills in the vicinity of where he was camped when he was arrested.

There is no authentic photograph of Crazy Horse. He refused to pose, saying: "Why would you wish to shorten my life by taking my shadow from me?"

Crazy Horse's last words to Agent Lee follow.

⟶ "We Preferred Our Own Way of Living"

My friend, I do not blame you for this. Had I listened to you this trouble would not have happened to me. I was not hostile to the white men. Sometimes my young men would attack the Indians who were their enemies and took their ponies. They did it in return.

We had buffalo for food, and their hides for clothing and for our teepees. We preferred hunting to a life of idleness on the reservation, where we were driven against our will. At times we did not get enough to eat, and we were not allowed to leave the reservation to hunt.

We preferred our own way of living. We were no expense to the government. All we wanted was peace and to be left alone. Soldiers were sent out in the winter, who destroyed our villages.

Then "Long Hair" (Custer) came in the same way. They say we massacred him, but he would have done the same thing to us had we not defended ourselves and fought to the last. Our first impulse was to escape with our squaws and papooses, but we were so hemmed in that we had to fight.

After that I went up on the Tongue River with a few of my people and lived in peace. But the government would not let me alone. Finally, I came back to the Red Cloud Agency. Yet I was not allowed to remain quiet.

I was tired of fighting. I went to the Spotted Tail Agency and asked that chief and his agent to let me live there in peace. I came here with the agent (Lee) to talk with the Big White

Chief but was not given a chance. They tried to confine me. I tried to escape, and a soldier ran his bayonet into me.

I have spoken.

Spotted Tail, Sioux, born 1823; died August 5, 1881.

Spotted Tail

SPOTTED TAIL was one of the most brilliant of the exceptional Sioux leaders. Raw courage and skill on the battlefield won his chieftain title from the hereditary claimant. His people, the Lower Brulé Sioux, recognized his leadership, and he took his place among the noted Sioux along with Red Cloud and Sitting Bull. He was a nephew of Crazy Horse.

Born in 1823 on the White River in South Dakota, Spotted Tail enjoyed the life and activities of the wide-ranging Sioux. As a young man he won his wife in a duel with a sub-chief. His action in warfare was outstanding.

He was chosen for important assignment by his people, made a trip to Washington, and was a guest of President Ulysses S. Grant. He met many important peace commissioners and army officers. As a negotiator he was dignified but affable. He was no great orator, but spoke effectively.

There was some distrust of his actions, however, and he was accused of selling part of the Sioux reservation and putting the proceeds to his own use. Red Cloud, on a speaking engagement in New York, accused Spotted Tail of duplicity. There was dissension on the reservation as well.

Spotted Tail had been selected for another trip to Washington, and this is thought to have set off action which resulted in a sub-chief shooting Spotted Tail to death. Crow Dog, a Sioux sub-chief, shot him with a rifle on August 5, 1881.

The speech below was made before a council meeting in 1877. Spotted Tail here shows a willingness to negotiate—one of the traits that had worked to his disadvantage.

My friends, your people have both intellect and heart; you use
these to consider in what way you can do the best to live. My
people, who are here before you, are precisely the same. I see
that my friends before me are men of age and dignity, and men
of that kind have good judgment and consider well what they
do. I infer from that, that you are here to consider what shall be
good for my people for a long time to come. I think each of you
has selected somewhere a good piece of land for himself with the
intention to live on it, that he may there raise his children. My
people are not different. We also live upon the earth and upon
the things that come to them from above. We have the same
thoughts and desires in that respect that the white people have.
This is the country where they were born, where they have
acquired all their property, their children and their horses. You
have come here to buy this country of us; and it would be well
if you would come with the goods you propose to give us, and
to put them out of your hand so we can see the good price you
propose to pay for it. Then our hearts would be glad.

My friends, when you go back to the Great Father, I want
you to tell him to send us goods; send us yokes and oxen, and
give us wagons so we can earn money by hauling goods from
the railroads. This seems to be a very hard day; half of our
country is at war, and we have come upon very difficult times.
This war did not spring up here in our land. It was brought upon
us by the children of the Great Father, who came to take our
land from us without price, and who do many evil things, the
Great Father and his children are to blame for this trouble. We
have here a storehouse to hold our provisions, but the Great
Father sent us very little provisions to put into our storehouse,
and when our people become displeased with our provisions

and have gone north to hunt, the children of the Great Father are fighting them. It has been our wish to live here peaceably, but the Great Father has filled it with soldiers who think only of our death. Some of our people who have gone from here in order that they may have a change, and others have been attacked by the soldiers from other directions; and now, that they are willing to come back, the soldiers stand between them and keep them from coming home. It seems to me there is a better way than this. When people come to trouble it is better for both parties to come together without arms, to talk it over, and find some peaceful way to settle.

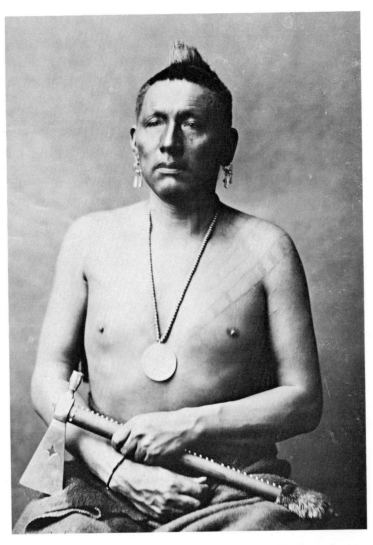

Governor Joe, Osage, birth date unknown; died 1883. Portrait possibly taken in Washington, D.C., about 1876.

Governor Joe

THE INDIAN orator was not lacking in skill as a satirist, and many were equipped with barbed tongues, as is evidenced by this incident. The speaker was Governor Joe, a chief of the Osages, whose name is given as Pa-I'm-No-Pa-She, or Not-Afraid-of-Longhairs. He was referred to as Big Hill Joe, because of his leadership of the group of Osages which was identified by this term. No birth date has been recorded. Governor Joe died in 1883.

As a representative of the Osages, Governor Joe attended a council at Fort Smith on September 13, 1865, when the United States Government sought to re-establish friendly relations with the Indians. Other tribes present at the council included the Cherokees, Creeks, Choctaws, Chickashas, Seminoles, Senecas, Shawnees, and Quapaws. By the fall of 1870, Governor Joe was recognized as the leader of the Osages.

Major Laban J. Miles in 1878 became agent to the Osages. His book, *Wah'Kon-Tah*, reminisces about his experiences, but dates of events are very vague. He writes "one morning," "some time later," "when payment time arrived," and "one afternoon." The anecdote related here no doubt developed as he wrote in his book, but no exact time can be determined. It is included as evidence that the Indians used sarcasm as well as flattery in their speeches.

Two young Osage braves had come into contact with a party of Wichita Indians and had killed a Wichita chief. The Wichitas were ready to go on the warpath, but the alert Indian agent was able to get them to meet the Osages to see if they could talk out some sort of arrangement that would appease the Wichitas and not anger the Osages. Following much talking, huffing and puffing, it appeared that the parley was stalemated.

223

Finally, the dignified Governor Joe stood up in the center of the assemblage, gathered his blanket around himself, and delivered the following blast. Wah'Kon-Tah as used in the quotation is defined as the Great Spirit.

"Osages Have Talked Like Blackbirds in Spring; Nothing Has Come from Their Hearts"

There have been many words. Wichitas have sent many words from their tongues; they have said little. Osages have talked like blackbirds in spring; nothing has come from their hearts. When Osages talk this way, Wichitas believe they are talkers like blackbird. I have listened long time to this talk of blackbirds, and I said when my people talk like blackbirds, Wichitas think they are women. I want to say few words, then Wichitas can go to their lodges and mourn for their chief. I want Wichitas to know this thing. I want them to know that Osage are great warriors. Today they have talked like women but they are warriors. They have those things which Wah'Kon-Tah gave to men, so that he could tell them from women. They know how to die in battle. I want Wichitas to know this thing. We will give ponies to Wichitas for this chief, then they can go home to their lodges. I have spoken.

Needless to say, the council broke up and the matter under discussion was considered settled.

Sitting Bull, Sioux, born 1834; died December 15, 1890. This is reported to be the last photograph of Sitting Bull, made in the latter
part of 1890.

Sitting Bull

SITTING BULL of the Sioux has been the inspiration of countless tales of fiction and fact, and it has been very difficult to separate the fiction from true fact. Only those who knew the Sioux and could merit their confidence were able to secure factual data upon which to base their writings. Probably the high-water mark in reporting on Sitting Bull was set by Stanley Vestal in his *Sitting Bull—Champion of the Sioux*. Vestal spent some five years gathering material for his book, and had such a mass of information that it was impossible to get anything but the very best into one volume. Vestal, in addition to spending much of his boyhood in Indian Territory, playing with Indian youths, and living with them for intervals, was adopted by Chief White Bull of the Sioux, who was an elder nephew of the famed Sitting Bull.

Sitting Bull was born in South Dakota in 1834. He was called a medicine man and a chief. He was above all a very shrewd leader and would have made a much more indelible mark upon western history had his warriors been equipped with better arms. As it turned out, he was laid low by the very people he had tried so hard to lead to a free and better life. He was murdered in the early morning of December 15, 1890, by Indian police who had been sent to arrest him. Reports indicate that plans called for arrest "dead or alive," with preference for bringing him in dead.

Sitting Bull was finally buried in a roughly made pine box, which was opened before burial so that chloride of lime and muriatic acid could be poured on his body before interment in the post cemetery at Fort Yates.

Thus ended the life of one of the greatest of all Indian leaders, whose reputation still is with us and whose exploits continue to inspire historians and writers.

A select committee from the United States Senate was appointed to make a study on the condition of the Indian tribes in the territories of Montana and Dakota, under a resolution adopted in the Senate in the spring of 1883. The committee members were H. L. Dawes of Massachusetts, John A. Logan of Illinois, Angus Cameron of Wisconsin, John T. Morgan of Alabama, and George G. Vest of Missouri.

While they were at the Standing Rock Agency in August of 1883, Sitting Bull was one of the Indians who appeared before the committee. Before Sitting Bull got down to the business of telling the committee what he thought about conditions of the Indians, this interesting repartee was entered in the official minutes:

Chairman: Ask Sitting Bull if he has anything to say to the committee.

Sitting Bull: Of course I will speak to you if you desire me to do so. I suppose it is only such men as you desire to speak who must say something.

Chairman: We supposed the Indians would select men to speak for them, but any man who desires to speak, or any man the Indians may desire shall talk for them. We will be glad to hear if he has anything to say.

Sitting Bull: Do you know who I am, that you speak of me as you do?

Chairman: I know that you are Sitting Bull, and if you have anything to say we will be glad to hear you.

Sitting Bull: Do you recognize me; do you know who I am?

Chairman: I know you are Sitting Bull.

Sitting Bull: You say you know I am Sitting Bull, but do you know the position I hold?

Chairman: I do not know any difference between you and the other Indians at this agency.

Sitting Bull: I am here by the will of the Great Spirit, and by his will I am a chief. My heart is red and sweet, and I know it is sweet, because whatever passes near me puts out its tongue to me; and yet you men have come here to talk with us, and you do not know who I am. I want to tell you that if the Great Spirit has chosen any one to be the chief of this country it is myself.

Later, Sitting Bull addressed the committee in this manner:

"I Feel That My Country Has Gotten a Bad Name"

I came in with a glad heart to shake hands with you, my friends, for I feel that I have displeased you. And here I am to apologize to you for my bad conduct and to take back what I said.

I will take it back because I consider I have made your hearts bad. I heard that you were coming here from the Great Father's house some time before you came, and I have been sitting here like a prisoner waiting for some one to release me. I was looking for you everywhere, and I considered that when we talked with you it was the same as if we were talking with the Great Father. And I believe that what I pour out from the heart the Great Father will hear.

What I take back is what I said to cause the people to leave the council, and want to apologize for leaving myself. The people acted like children, and I am sorry for it. I was very sorry when I found out that your intentions were good and entirely different from what I supposed they were.

Now I will tell you my mind and I will tell everything straight. I know the Great Spirit is looking down upon me from above, and will hear what I say, therefore I will do my best to talk straight. And I am in hopes that some one will listen to my wishes and help me to carry them out.

I have always been a chief, and have been made chief of all the land. Thirty-two years ago I was present at the councils with the white man, and at the time of the Fort Rice council I was on the prairie listening to it. And since then a great many questions have been asked me about it, and I always said, wait. And then the Black Hills council was held, and they asked me to give up that land, and I said they must wait. I remember well all the promises that were made about that land because I have thought a great deal about them since that time.

229

Of course, I know that the Great Spirit provided me with animals for my food, but I did not stay out on the prairie because I did not wish to accept the offers of the Great Father, for I sent in a great many of my people and I told them that the Great Father was providing for them and keeping his agreements with them. And I was sending the Indians word all the time I was out that they must remember their agreements and fulfill them, and carry them out straight.

When the English authorities were looking for me I heard that the Great Father's people were looking for me, too. I was not lost. I knew where I was going all the time. Previous to that time, when a Catholic priest called "White Hair" (meaning Bishop Marty) came to see me, I told him all these things plainly. He told me the wishes of the Great Father, and I made promises which I meant to fulfill, and did fulfill. And when I went over into the British possessions he followed me, and I told him everything that was in my heart, and sent him back to tell the Great Father what I told him.

And General Terry sent me word afterwards to come in, because he had big promises to make me. And I sent him word that I would not throw my country away; that I considered it all mine still, and I wanted him to wait just four years for me; that I had gone over there to attend to some business of my own, and my people were doing just as any other people would do. If a man loses anything and goes back and looks carefully for it he will find it, and that is what the Indians are doing now when they ask you to give them the things that were promised them in the past. And I do not consider that they should be treated like beasts, and that is the reason I have grown up with the feelings I have.

Whatever you wanted of me I have obeyed, and I have come when you called me. The Great Father sent me word that whatever he had against me in the past had been forgiven and thrown aside, and he would have nothing against me in the future, and I accepted his promises and came in. And he told me not to step aside from the white man's path, and I told him I would not, and I am doing my best to travel in that path.

I feel that my country has gotten a bad name, and I want it to have a good name. It used to have a good name, and I sit sometimes and wonder who it is that has given it a bad name. You are the only people now who can give it a good name, and I want you to take good care of my country and respect it.

When we sold the Black Hills we got a very small price for it, and not what we ought to have received. I used to think that the size of the payments would remain the same all the time, but they are growing smaller all the time.

I want you to tell the Great Father everything I have said, and that we want some benefits from the promises he has made to us. And I don't think I should be tormented with anything about giving up any part of my land until those promises are fulfilled. I would rather wait until that time, when I will be ready to transact any business he may desire.

I consider that my country takes in the Black Hills, and runs from the Powder River to the Missouri, and that all of this land belongs to me. Our reservation is not as large as we want it to be, and I suppose the Great Father owes us money now for land he has taken from us in the past.

You white men advise us to follow your ways, and therefore I talk as I do. When you have a piece of land, and anything trespasses on it, you catch it and keep it until you get damages, and I am doing the same thing now. And I want you to tell this to the Great Father for me. I am looking into the future for the benefit of my children, and that is what I mean, when I say I want my country taken care of for me.

My children will grow up here, and I am looking ahead for their benefit, and for the benefit of my children's children, too;

and even beyond that again. I sit here and look around me now, and I see my people starving, and I want the Great Father to make an increase in the amount of food that is allowed us now, so that they may be able to live. We want cattle to butcher—I want to kill 300 head of cattle at a time. That is the way you live, and we want to live the same way. This is what I want you to tell the Great Father when you go back home.

If we get the things we want, our children will be raised like the white children. When the Great Father told me to live like his people I told him to send me six teams of mules, because that is the way white people make a living, and I wanted my children to have these things to help them to make a living. I also told him to send me two spans of horses with wagons, and everything else my children would need. I also asked for a horse and buggy for my children. I was advised to follow the ways of the white man, and that is why I asked for those things.

I never ask for anything that is not needed. I also asked for a cow and a bull for each family, so that they can raise cattle of their own. I asked for four yokes of oxen and wagons with them. Also a yoke of oxen and a wagon for each of my children to haul wood with.

It is your own doing that I am here. You sent me here, and advised me to live as you do, and it is not right for me to live in poverty. I asked the Great Father for hogs, male and female, and for male and female sheep for my children to raise from. I did not leave out anything in the way of animals that the white men have; I asked for every one of them. I want you to tell the Great Father to send me some agricultural implements, so that I will not be obliged to work bare-handed.

Whatever he sends to this agency our agent will take care of for us, and we will be satisfied because we know he will keep everything right. Whatever is sent here for us he will be pleased to take care of for us. I want to tell you that our rations have been reduced to almost nothing, and many of the people have starved to death.

Now I beg of you to have the amount of rations increased so that our children will not starve, but will live better than they do now. I want clothing, too, and I will ask for that, too. We want all kinds of clothing for our people. Look at the men around here and see how poorly dressed they are. We want some clothing this month, and when it gets cold we want more to protect us from the weather.

That is all I have to say.

Sitting Bull has been the subject of many books and articles, and opinions on his life are varied. There is no doubt, however, that he was dedicated to the Sioux Indians and his thoughts were for their welfare. C. A. Eastman, as quoted in Stanley Vestal's *Sitting Bull—Champion of the Sioux*, says "He was no medicine man, but a statesman, one of the most far-sighted we have had."

Sitting Bull's interest in the welfare of his people is shown by this speech which he made at a Catholic school on the reservation. The invitation to talk to the young Indians was made by the Reverend Mr. Jerome Hunt. Here is what he said on that occasion:

"You Are Living in a New Path"

My dear grandchildren: All of your folks are my relatives, because I am a Sioux, and so are they. I was glad to hear that the Black Robe had given you this school where you can learn to read, write, and count the way white people do. You are also being taught a new religion. You are shown how the white men work and make things. You are living in a new path.

When I was your age, things were entirely different. I had no teachers but my parents and relatives. They are dead and gone now, and I am left alone. It will be the same with you. Your parents are aging and will die some day, leaving you alone.

So it is for you to make something of yourselves, and this can only be done while you are young.

In my early days I was eager to learn and to do things, and therefore I learned quickly, and that made it easier for my teachers. Now I often pick up papers and books which have all kinds of pictures and marks on them, but I cannot understand them as a white person does. They have a way of communicating by the use of written symbols and figures; but before they could do that, they had to have an understanding among themselves. You are learning that, and I was very much pleased to hear you reading.

In future your business dealings with the whites are going to be very hard, and it behooves you to learn well what you are taught here. But that is not all. We older people need you. In our dealings with the white men, we are just the same as blind men, because we do not understand them. We need you to help us understand what the white men are up to. My Grandchildren, be good. Try and make a mark for yourselves. Learn all you can.

With all my heart I thank my Black Robe friends for their goodness and kindness towards me.

Geronimo, Apache, born 1829; died February 17, 1909. This picture was made in March, 1886, before the escape of the noted Chiracahua Apache chief from prison.

Geronimo

GERONIMO was born at the headwaters of the Gila River, in New Mexico, in 1829. As leader of the Apache Indians in Southwestern United States, he made a record of ferocity and tenacity seldom equaled in the Indian wars. Outmanned and outgunned, he was able to outmaneuver all of the troops sent after him.

Geronimo believed in the old adage of "he who fights and runs away, lives to fight another day," and that is the tactic by which his small group of Apache warriors was able to harass such a large area of the Southwest. They would strike and then fade into the mountainous country, making their next foray miles from the last one. Geronimo was captured several times, but always escaped and resumed his wild life. He finally surrendered at Camp Bowie, Arizona, on September 4, 1886. At the end there were some five thousand troops after a band of thirty-six Apaches, including men, women, and children.

As a prisoner of war, Geronimo and other Apaches were sent to Fort Pickens, Pensacola, Florida; then to Mount Vernon, Alabama; and finally to Fort Sill, Oklahoma, where he died from pneumonia on February 17, 1909. He is buried at the fort.

Geronimo was an attraction to the numerous visitors at Fort Sill. He was converted to Christianity in 1903. He went to Washington, D.C., in 1905, and was a conspicuous part of the inaugural procession of President Theodore Roosevelt.

Geronimo was an able speaker and the talk given here was at a conference held March 25, 1886, at the Canon of the Funnels, near San Bernardino Springs, New Mexico, where General George Crook was attempting to deal with the Chiricahua Apache chieftains. Geronimo was trying to impress Crook with his good intentions.

I want to talk first of the causes which led me to leave the reservation. I was living quietly and contented, doing and thinking of no harm, while at the Sierra Blanca. I don't know what harm I did to those three men, Chato, Mickey Free, and Lieutenant Davis. I was living peaceably and satisfied when people began to speak bad of me. I should be glad to know who started those stories. I was living peaceably with my family, having plenty to eat, sleeping well, taking care of my people, and perfectly contented. I don't know where those bad stories first came from. There we were doing well and my people well. I was behaving well. I hadn't killed a horse or man, American or Indian. I don't know what was the matter with the people in charge of us. They knew this to be so, and yet they said I was a bad man and the worst man there; but what harm had I done? I was living peaceably and well, but I did not leave on my own accord. Had I left it would have been right to blame me; but as it is, blame those men who started this talk about me.

Some time before I left an Indian named Wodiskay had a talk with me. He said, "they are going to arrest you," but I paid no attention to him, knowing that I had done no wrong; and the wife of Mangus, "Huera," told me that they were going to seize me and put me and Mangus in the guard-house, and I learned from the American and Apache soldiers, from Chato, and Mickey Free, that the Americans were going to arrest me and hang me, and so I left.

I would like to know now who it was that gave the order to arrest me and hang me. I was living peaceably there with my family under the shade of the trees, doing just what General Crook had told me I must do and trying to follow his advice. I want to know now who it was ordered me to be arrested. I was praying to the light and to the darkness, to God and to the sun, to let me live quietly with my family. I don't know what the reason was that people should speak badly of me. I don't want to be blamed. The fault was not mine. Blame those three men. With them is the fault, and find out who it was that began that bad talk about me.

I have several times asked for peace, but trouble has come from the agents and interpreters. I don't want what has passed to happen again. Now, I am going to tell you something else. The Earth-Mother is listening to me and I hope that all may be so arranged that from now on there shall be no trouble and that we shall always have peace. Whenever we see you coming to where we are, we think it is God—you must come always with God. From this on I do not want that anything shall be told you about me even in joke. Whenever I have broken out, it was always been on account of bad talk. From this on I hope that people will tell me nothing but the truth. From this on I want to do what is right and nothing else and I do not want you to believe any bad papers about me. I want the papers sent you to tell the truth about me, because I want to do what is right. Very often there are stories put in the newspapers that I am to be hanged. I don't want that any more. When a man tries to do right, such stories ought not to be put in the newspapers.

There are very few of my men left now. They have done some bad things but I want them all rubbed out now and let us never speak of them again. There are very few of us left. We think of our relations, brothers, brothers-in-law, father-in-law, etc., over on the reservation, and from this on we want to live at peace just as they are doing, and to behave as they are behaving. Sometimes a man does something and men are sent out to bring in his head. I don't want such things to happen to us. I don't want that we should be killing each other.

What is the matter that you don't speak to me? It would be

better if you would speak to me and look with a pleasant face. It would make better feeling. I would be glad if you did. I'd be better satisfied if you would talk to me once in a while. Why don't you look at me and smile at me? I am the same man; I have the same feet, legs, and hands, and the sun looks down on me a complete man. I want you to look and smile at me.

I have not forgotten what you told me, although a long time has passed. I keep it in my memory. I am a complete man. Nothing has gone from my body. From here on I want to live at peace. Don't believe any bad talk you hear about me. The agents and the interpreter hear that somebody has done wrong, and they blame it all on me. Don't believe what they say. I don't want any of this bad talk in the future. I don't want those men who talked this way about me to be my agents any more. I want good men to be my agents and interpreters; people who will talk right. I want this peace to be legal and good. Whenever I meet you I talk good to you, and you to me, and peace is soon established; but when you go to the reservation you put agents and interpreters over us who do bad things. Perhaps they don't mind what you tell them, because I do not believe you would tell them to do bad things to us. In the future we don't want these bad men to be allowed near where we are to live. We don't want any more of that kind of bad talk. I don't want any man who will talk bad about me, and tell lies, to be there, because I am going to try and live well and peaceably. I want to have a good man put over me.

While living I want to live well. I know I have to die sometime, but even if the heavens were to fall on me, I want to do what is right. I think I am a good man, but in the papers all over the world they say I am a bad man; but it is a bad thing to say so about me. I never do wrong without a cause. Every day I am thinking, how am I to talk to you to make you believe what I say; and, I think, too, that you are thinking of what you are to say to me. There is one God looking down on us all. We are all children of the one God. God is listening to me. The sun, the darkness, the winds, are all listening to what we now say.

To prove to you that I am telling you the truth, remember I sent you word that I would come from a place far away to speak to you here, and you see us now. Some have come on horseback and some on foot. If I were thinking bad, or if I had done bad, I would never have come here. If it has been my fault, would I have come so far to talk to you? I have told you all that has happened. I also had feared that I should never see Ka-e-te-na again, but here he is, and I want the past to be buried. I am glad to see Ka-e-te-na. I was afraid I should never see him again. That was one reason, too, why I left. I wish that Ka-e-te-na would be returned to us to live with his family. I now believe what I was told. Now I believe that all told me is true, because I see Ka-e-te-na again. I am glad to see him again, as I was told I should. We are all glad. My body feels good because I see Ka-e-te-na, and my breathing is good. Now I can eat well, drink well, sleep well, and be glad. I can go everywhere with good feeling. Now, what I want is peace in good faith. Both you and I think well and think alike.

Well, we have talked enough and set here long enough. I may have forgotten something, but if I remember it, I will tell you of it tonight, or tomorrow, or some other time. I have finished for today, but I'll have something more to say bye and bye.

Kicking Bear, Dakota: Miniconjou, born 1853; died May 28, 1904.
Portrait taken in 1896.

Kicking Bear

KICKING BEAR gained his notoriety from his participation in and leadership of the Ghost Dance movement among the Sioux Indians in the period around 1890. This religion was started in Utah in the year 1888 by Wovoka, a Piute Indian, and within two years had spread over most of the western half of the United States. Kicking Bear had been a member of a delegation sent to Utah by the Sioux, and upon his return to the reservation became active in exhorting the Indians in the ritual of the Ghost Dance.

Records indicate that Kicking Bear was born in 1853, but the place of birth is unknown. His father was named Black Fox, and his mother's name was Wood Pecker. He was a husky, vigorous man. Kicking Bear died May 28, 1904, and he may be buried in the vicinity of Manderson, South Dakota. This would make his age at his death about fifty-one years.

Kicking Bear married a niece of a Minneconjou chief, and paid the marriage price with horses which he had taken from the Crow Indians, who were always at odds with the Sioux. By his marriage to the niece of a chief, Kicking Bear became a minor band chief in the Sioux Nation, but he attracted the most attention by his advocacy of the Ghost Dance.

In order to relieve tension among the Indians following the decline of the Ghost Dance activity, a group of prominent Sioux was sent to Europe to tour with Buffalo Bill's Wild West Show. Cody was touring Europe in 1890, and returned to the States that winter. Cody left Philadelphia on April 1, 1891, to return to his circus, taking with him a group of Indians which included Kicking Bear. The Indians were a major attraction of the Wild West Show. Little was heard of Kicking Bear after his return from the tour.

243

The speech given here was delivered in 1890 to a council of Sioux Indians, with no whites present. Major James McLaughlin asked Short Bull, another Sioux, who had attended the council, to repeat what Kicking Bear had said. A phenomenon of Indian oratory was the amazing memory of the speaker and the ability of the listener to remember what was said. Short Bull lost no time in passing along the speech, and McLaughlin wrote it down.

The speech was included in Major McLaughlin's book *My Friend the Indian*, and extensive search has not revealed it printed elsewhere. The Major included it to show the willingness of the Indians to believe in almost anything that promised to remove the white man from their land. McLaughlin certainly was in a position to evaluate the speech, and while it was absurd, it showed inventiveness on the part of the speaker, who undoubtedly held his listeners under his spell.

Permission to use this material has been granted by Robert C. McLaughlin, a grandson of the widely known Indian agent.

"I Bring You Word from Your Fathers the Ghosts"

My brothers, I bring to you the promise of a day in which there will be no white man to lay his hand on the bridle of the Indian's horse; when the red men of the prairie will rule the world and not be turned from the hunting grounds by any man. I bring you word from your fathers the ghosts, that they are now marching to join you, led by the Messiah who came once to live on earth with the white men, but was cast out and killed by them. I have seen the wonders of the spirit-land, and have talked with the ghosts. I traveled far and am sent back with a message to tell you to make ready for the coming of the Messiah and return of the ghosts in the spring.

In my teepee on the Cheyenne reservation I arose after the corn-planting, sixteen moons ago, and prepared for my journey. I had seen many things and had been told by a voice to go forth and meet the ghosts, for they were to return and inhabit the earth. I traveled far on the cars of the white men, until I came to the place where the railroad stopped. There I met two men, Indians, whom I had never seen before, but who greeted me as a brother and gave me meat and bread. They had three horses, and we rode without talking for four days, for I knew they were to be witnesses to what I should see. Two suns had we traveled, and had passed the last signs of the white man—for no white man had ever had the courage to travel so far—when we saw a strange and fierce-looking black man, dressed in skins. He was living alone, and had medicine with which he could do what he wished. He would wave his hands and make great heaps of money; another motion, and we saw many spring wagons, already painted and ready to hitch horses to; yet another motion of the hands, and there sprung before us great herds of buffalo. The black man spoke and told us that he was the friend of the Indian; that we should remain with him and go no farther, and we might take what we wanted of the money, and spring wagons, and the buffalo. But our hearts were turned away from the black man, my brothers, and we left him and traveled for two days more.

On the evening of the fourth day, when we were weak and faint from our journey, we looked for a camping place, and were met by a man dressed like an Indian, but whose hair was long and glistening like the yellow money of the white man. His face was very beautiful to see, and when he spoke my heart was glad and I forgot my hunger and the toil I had gone through. And he said, "How, my children. You have done well to make this long journey to come to me. Leave your horses and follow me." And our hearts sang in our breasts and we were glad. He led the way up a great ladder of small clouds, and we followed him up through an opening in the sky. My brothers, the tongue of Kicking Bear is straight and he cannot tell all that he saw, for he is not an orator, but the forerunner and herald of the ghosts. He whom we followed took us to the Great Spirit and his wife, and we lay prostrate on the ground, but I saw that they were dressed as Indians. Then from an opening in the sky we were shown all the countries of the earth and the camping grounds of our fathers since the beginning; all were there, the teepees, and the ghosts of our fathers, and great herds of buffalo, and a country that smiled because it was rich and the white man was not there. Then he whom we had followed showed us his hands and feet, and there were wounds in them which had been made by the whites when he went to them and they crucified him. And he told us that he was going to come again on earth, and this time he would remain and live with the Indians, who were his chosen people.

Then we were seated on rich skins, of animals unknown to me, before the open door of the teepee of the Great Spirit, and told how to say the prayers and perform the dances I am now come to show my brothers. And the Great Spirit spoke to us saying:

Take this message to my red children and tell it to them as I say it. I have neglected the Indians for many moons, but I will make them my people now if they obey me in this message. The earth is getting old, and I will make it new for my chosen people, the Indians, who are to inhabit it, and among them will be all those of their ancestors who have died, their fathers, mothers, brothers, cousins and wives—all those who hear my voice and my words through the tongues of my children.

I will cover the earth with new soil to a depth of five times the height of a man, and under this new soil will be buried all the whites, and all the holes and the rotten places will be filled up. The new lands will be covered with sweet-grass and running water and trees, and herds of buffalo and ponies will stray over it, that my red children may eat and drink, hunt and rejoice. And the sea to the west I will fill up so that no ships may pass over it, and the other seas will I make impassable. And while I am making the new earth the Indians who have heard this message and who dance and pray and believe will be taken up in the air and suspended there, while the wave of new earth is passing; then set down among the ghosts of their ancestors, relatives and friends. Those of my children who doubt will be left in undesirable places, where they will be lost and wander around until they believe and learn the songs and the dance of the ghosts.

And while my children are dancing and making ready to join the ghosts, they shall have no fear of the white man, for I will take from the white man the secret of making gunpowder, and the powder they now have on hand will not burn when it is directed against the red people, my children, who know the songs and dances of the ghosts; but that powder which my children, the red men, have, will burn and kill when it is directed against the whites and used by those who believe. And if a red man die at the hands of the whites while he is dancing, his spirit will only go to the end of the earth and there join the ghosts of his father and return to his friends in the spring. Go then, my children, and tell these things to all the people and make all ready for the coming of the ghosts.

We were given food that was rich and sweet to taste, and as we sat there eating, there came up through the clouds a man, tall as a tree and thin like a snake, with great teeth sticking out of his mouth, his body covered with short hair, and we knew at once it was the Evil Spirit. And he said to the Great Spirit, "I want half the people of the earth." And the Great Spirit answered and said, "No, I cannot give you any; I love them all too much." The Evil Spirit asked again and was again refused, and asked the third time, and the Great Spirit told him that he could have the whites to do what he liked with, but that he would not let him have any Indians, as they were his chosen people for all future time. Then we were shown the dances and taught the songs that I am bringing to you, my brothers, and were led down the ladder of clouds by him who had taken us up. We found our horses and rode back to the railroad, the Messiah flying along in the air with us and teaching us the songs for the new dances. At the railroad he left us and told us to return to our people, and

247

tell them, and all the people of the red nations, what we had seen; and he promised us that he would return to the clouds no more, but would remain at the end of the earth and lead the ghosts of our fathers to meet us when the next winter is passed.

Quanah Parker, Comanche, born 1845; died February 23, 1911.
This portrait was taken in an early-day studio.

Quanah Parker

THE COMANCHE Indians were described as the Lords of the Plains, and under their brave and resourceful chiefs they ravaged the High Plains from the Platte River down into Mexico. One of the most distinguished chiefs of this proud people was Quanah Parker. Quanah had an unusual background. He was the son of a Comanche chief and a white woman, Cynthia Ann Parker. Cynthia was taken from Parker's Fort on the Navasota River in East Texas at the age of nine, when the Comanches raided the fort and left only a few survivors.

Quanah was born in 1845, although the stone erected over his grave gives the date as 1852. He died February 23, 1911, and was buried in Post Oak Cemetery, near the mission of the same name.

Quanah's band of Comanches, the Kwahadi, refused to go onto the reservation following the Treaty of 1867. About seven hundred Indians were with Quanah at the famed Battle of Adobe Walls, in West Texas. This started a series of border rampages along the southern edge of Kansas that lasted for years. In 1876 Quanah finally led his band in to Fort Sill, Oklahoma, where they surrendered and submitted to reservation life. Quanah made the best of the new conditions, and was the most prominent and influential member of the confederation of Comanche, Cheyenne, and Kiowa tribes which settled in the neighborhood of Fort Sill.

The City of Quanah, Texas, was named for him. Quanah has many relatives living in Oklahoma.

The speech below was made to Captain Hugh L. Scott, and the language is that set down during the 1890's. It describes action and events leading up to the Adobe Walls fight.

251

A long time ago I had a friend killed by the Tonkawas on Double Mountain Fork of the Brazos. That make me feel bad. We had grown up together, gone to war together. We were all very sorry that man was killed. The Tonkawa killed him—it make my heart hot. I want to make it even.

At that time I was a pretty big young man and knew how to fight pretty good. I work for one month trying to get Comanches to go to war with me. I go to the Nokoni camp first, on head of Cache Creek. I call in everybody. I tell them my friend he killed in Texas. I fill pipe, I say to man, "You want to smoke?" He take pipe and smoke. I give pipe to other men. One man say, "I do not want to smoke. If I smoke pipe, I go to war." I say, "You not excused. God kill you if you be afraid."

I go see Kiowas on Elk Creek, then Quahadis, then I go see Cheyennes. Lots of them smoke pipe. Cheyenne camp on Washita near where Fort Elliott later built, where Washita forks around hill. Lots of Comanches there—Otter Belt, He Bear (Parra-o-coom), Tabananica, Old Man Esa Rose (White Wolf). Camps in different places.

They say, "When you go to war, Quanah?"

I say, "Maybe tomorrow, maybe next day. Have big dance tonight. Big Horse Society dance here; Little Horse Society dance there; Fox Quirts on this side."

Then I hear somebody call, "Quanah, the old men want to see you over here!" I see Old Man Otter Belt, White Wolf, and lots of other old men.

They say, "You pretty good fighter, Quanah, but you not know everything. We think better you take pipe first against white buffalo killers. You kill them first and make your heart feel good. After that you come back, take all the young men, go to war, Texas!"

I say, "Otter Belt and He Bear, you take pipe yourself, after I take young men to go to Texas."

They say, "All right."

Isatai make big talk at that time. He says, "God tell me we going to kill lots of white men. I stop bullets in their guns. Bullets not pierce our shirts. We kill all, just like old women. God told me the truth."

Before that Isatai was pretty good medicine man, make pretty good medicine. He had sat down far away and listen. God tell him, "Maybeso on little creek, fifty miles away, is white soldiers. We must go kill them." This time he listen to what God tell him.

Soon was move to Fort Elliott—no got fort there at this time. I pick seven scouts to go look for white men's adobe houses on Canadian. Old Man White Wolf go with them. They gone all night. Next day our watchers on a little hill call out, "Here they come!" We see our scouts circle four times to right and know they find the houses. Our whole village, the women and children and everybody, make a long line in front of the camp, Old Man Black Beard in the middle. Then the seven scouts come in single file in front of Black Beard.

He ask, "Tell the truth, what did you see?"

First scout say, "I see four log houses. I see horses moving about." All scouts say the same thing.

Black Beard say, "All right. Pretty soon we kill some white men."

Everybody saddled up, took their war bonnets and shields. We started when sun there (about eleven), we stopped when sun there (about four). We took off the saddles and blankets from our horses, hobbled the extra horses, make medicine, paint faces, put on war bonnets, then move in fours across the Canadian at sundown. We kept along the river to pretty near Red Hill near Adobe Creek, where houses were. We walk our horses, because enemy could hear horses trotting a long way off.

253

At dark some men want to go to sleep. He Bear say, "Dismount. Hold lariats in your hands. When I call, you mount again."

While we wait, some sleep, some smoke and talk. Finally He Bear and Tabananica call them, "Everybody mount." All mount again and travel until there is just a little daylight. Pretty soon we make a line. All the chiefs try to hold the young men back: "You go too fast. No good to go so fast."

Pretty soon the chiefs call, "All right. Go ahead!" We charge pretty fast on our horses, throwing up dust. Many prairie dog holes. I see men and horses roll over and over. Some men who were ahead drove off the white men's horses.

I was in the middle of the line. I got up into the adobe houses with another Comanche. We poked holes through the roof to shoot. Two white men killed in wagon. I not see any other killed. Four Cheyenne, some Arapahoes and Comanches killed. My first wife's father got leg broken by bullet. I got shot in side.

That pretty big fight. Lasted from sunrise to midday. Then we go back. All Cheyennes heap mad at Isatai, tell him, "What's the matter your medicine? You got polecat medicine!"

One Comanche killed was a yellow nigger painted like Comanche. He had left nigger soldiers' company, everybody know that (deserter from the Tenth Cavalry).

Pretty soon we all go back, get saddles, go to village. I take all young men, go war Texas.

Quanah Parker's mother, Cynthia Ann Parker, was buried in Texas, and many years later the remains were exhumed and taken to Oklahoma, where they were buried in Post Oak Cemetery, near the famous Star House in which Quanah lived. This cemetery was near the Post Oak Mission. Quanah was also buried in the same plot. His gravestone reads, "Resting here until day breaks and shadows fall and darkness disappears," but his remains were moved to Fort Sill. As the Fort Sill military establishment began the use of long range artillery, this ground was taken into the Post's artillery range, and all the Indian graves were moved.

On the occasion of the reburial of Cynthia Ann's remains, Quanah made a short talk at the graveside. He spoke in broken English, but with deep feeling, saying:

"I Want My People Follow After White Way"

Forty years ago my mother died. She captured by Comanche, nine years old. Love Indian and wild life so well no want to go back to white folks. All same people, God say. I love my mother. I like white people. Got great heart. I want my people follow after white way, get educate, know work, make living when payments stop. I tell um they got to know pick cotton, plow corn. I want um know white man's God. Comanche may die tomorrow, or ten years. When end come then they all be together again. I want to see my mother again. That's why when Government United States give money for new grave I have this funeral and ask white folks to help bury. Glad to see so many my people here at funeral. That's all.

Quanah made a visit to Oklahoma City, Oklahoma, and on October 24, 1910, gave a talk before a group in that city. He makes reference to the removal of his mother from Texas to the family plot in Oklahoma, and also gives some explanation of the actions of his people. He mentions also his investment in an early day railroad in Western Oklahoma and Texas. The Burk Burnett mentioned was a Texas rancher upon whose land a fabulous oil field was developed and for whom the town of Burkburnett, Texas, was named.

Here is what Quanah said:

"Some White People Do That, Too"

Now, Ladies and Gentlemen, you read the paper. Me move from Texas over Oklahoma, my country. I see John Stephens, Congress from Texas, and I tell him would like him get bill

$1,000.00 to remove my mother remains two years ago. Bill passed and after that somebody, New York man, started that bill, and last June I been to Washington. I come again and see about it. Made bill $800.00. I used $200.00 buy new coffin. Now, ladies and gentlemen, Texas objects me do that. I have over at my home my oldest son dead, some seven or eight years ago. Nobody knows when me die, maybe tomorrow or ten years, but me have family graveyard and me want bury my mother there now, here is another thing. Here is all of my acquaintances come from Quanah. They came from my town, the Quanah country. All that used to be my hunting ground, snakes up there. My town up there wanted to put railroad west of Quanah. They came to me and I helped them out. I invested $40,000.00 in Quanah Western. I wanted to run it over New Mexico.

Well, you see here this night what I want to tell you now. I got one good friend, Burk Burnett. He big-hearted, rich cowman. Help my people good deal. You see big man hold tight to money, afraid to die. Burnett helped anybody. I came from Fort Sill. No ride me in like horse or cow. Had a big war; I fought General McKenzie; he used two thousand men. I had four hundred and fifty men. I used this knife. I see eight miles perhaps, lots of soldiers coming. I say, "Hold on, no go over there." Maybe we go at night, maybe stampede soldiers' horses first. I strew my men around in circle and tell them, "Holler." I gathered maybe three hundred fifty United States horses that night. You see how bad me that time. The next morning they came up my trail. I ready to fight, came up our trail, lot men. Way head of it maybe fifty or sixty men. I tell my men to stand up behind hill, holler, shoot and run. I run to one side and use this knife. I came up right side, kill man, sergeant, and scalp. You see how bad me at that time. Well, ladies and gentlemen, now I working for Government. I work for my Indians. Every year me want to go to Washington and I work for my Indians. Put young Indians in school, and make Indians do like white man. They have horses like white man. Some Indians no good, you see man buy bottle whiskey and play cards. That reason some men no good. Some white people do that, too.

Appendix

"An Indian's Views of Indian Affairs," by Chief Joseph

The *North American Review* in its issue of April, 1879, printed a speech made by Chief Joseph of the Nez Percés under the title, "An Indian's Views of Indian Affairs." This has been one of the most widely quoted speeches made by any of the Indian orators, but the pity of it is that usually only excerpts have been given.

Following his attempts to get relief from Congress and the Department of Indian Affairs, Joseph was permitted to go to Washington in January, 1879. There, on January 14, he appeared before a large gathering of cabinet members, congressmen, diplomats, and others, and presented his plea for relief for his people. He was eloquent in pleading the cause of the Nez Percés, telling of their need for a healthful place to live, their need for more food and medicine, and their right to be considered as equal to other citizens of the United States.

Joseph detailed the Nez Percés' flight across the rugged mountains of Idaho, Wyoming, and Montana, and the victories his small group won over four different army generals, and then of the difficult decision to surrender in order to save his people further death and suffering.

Little did they know that the agreement made with General Nelson A. Miles at surrender would not be fulfilled. Joseph expressed consternation with the indecision of government. He showed contempt for General O. O. Howard, who had first shown contempt for the Indians.[1] While Joseph surrendered to General Miles, the

[1] The people referred to in Joseph's talk are further identified as: President Rutherford B. Hayes, who was in office at the time of Joseph's speech in Washington (the trouble had arisen during the tenure of President U. S. Grant);

tone of his remarks regarding Miles is different from the comments recounting Howard's action against the Nez Percés.

A torrent of material has been written about Joseph's conduct of the "Nez Percé War" but probably the best all-around account of the troubles and the action is given by Alvin M. Josephy, Jr., in *The Nez Perce Indians and the Opening of the Northwest*.

The full speech, as printed in the *Review*, is reproduced here.

My friends, I have been asked to show you my heart. I am glad to have a chance to do so. I want the white people to understand my people. Some of you think an Indian is like a wild animal. This is a great mistake. I will tell you all about our people, and then you can judge whether an Indian is a man or not. I believe much trouble and blood would be saved if we opened our hearts more. I will tell you in my way how the Indian sees things. The white man has more words to tell you how they look to him, but it does not require many words to speak the truth. What I have to say will come from my heart, and I will speak with a straight tongue. Ah-cum-kin-i-ma-me-hut (the Great Spirit) is looking at me, and will hear me.

My name is In-mut-too-yah-lat-lat (Thunder traveling over the Mountains). I am chief of the Wal-lam-wat-kin band of Chute-pa-lu, or Nez Percés (nose-pierced Indians). I was born in eastern Oregon, thirty-eight winters ago. My father was chief before me. When a young man, he was called Joseph by Mr. Spaulding, a missionary. He died a few years ago. He left a good name on earth. He advised me well for my people.

Our fathers gave us many laws, which they had learned from their fathers. These laws were good. They told us to treat all

---

Carl Schurz, Secretary of the Interior; E. A. Hayt, Commissioner of Indian Affairs; General John Gibbon; General Samuel D. Sturgis; General John O'Neil was an Indian Inspector; Colonel William Stickney, a member of the Board of Indian Commissioners; Governor Isaac I. Stevens, the first governor of the Washington Territory; Rev. Mr. Henry H. Spaulding, and his wife, Elisa, Presbyterian missionaries; Arthur I. Chapman, a friend of Joseph's; probably Henry C. Johnson, a citizen volunteer.